D0790189

Paths to improvement

Navigating your way to success

Robert W. Eichinger, Michael M. Lombardo, Alex J. Stiber, J. Evelyn Orr

Paths to improvement

Navigating your way to success

(Formerly known as Broadband Talent Management™: Paths to Improvement)

www.kornferry.com

ISBN 978-1-933578-31-6 • Print

Item number 82123 • Print

Paths to improvement
Navigating your way to success

Printings:

Broadband Talent Management™: Paths to Improvement	version 05.1a 1st—05/05
	version 05.1a 2nd—06/05
	version 05.1a 3rd—03/06
	version 05.1a 4th—11/07
	version 05.1a 5th—12/09
	version 05.1a 6th—09/10
Paths to improvement: Navigating your way to success	version 11.1a 1st—03/11
	version 11.1a 2nd—11/11
	version 11.1a 3rd—06/12
	version 11.1a 4th—03/13
	version 11.1a 5th—11/13
	version 11.1a 6th—10/14
	version 11.1b 7th—07/15

Table of contents

Introduction

Work, like life, is an exercise in navigation. Whether you are guided by compass, GPS, street signs, or stars, two key pieces of information are essential in order to navigate your way: where you are now and where you want to be.

Imagine an interactive map for your career. Once you know where you are and where you want to be, the methods for *how* you reach your destination are numerous. Some routes will be direct, others less direct. Some routes will be safe, others more risky. How long it takes to get there is another factor to consider. It can be tempting to choose the most familiar path, but the goal is to choose a path that will get you to your destination.

For most people, development has meant discovering and fixing weaknesses. While this approach can work, focusing exclusively on fixing weaknesses can be challenging and discouraging. Creating a "fix-it" development plan is not always the most effective route to improvement. In fact, most development plans (if they exist at all) are poorly crafted, unlikely to be executed, and have variable outcomes. Fortunately, development plans are not the only way to accomplish a goal or get results.

So, if converting your weaknesses to strengths is not the panacea, what other paths are available to help you improve?

Paths to improvement: Navigating your way to success is designed for individuals who are seeking alternative routes to improve their performance and potential. It is also for coaches, mentors, bosses, and HR professionals— anyone helping others improve their effectiveness. This book reviews 14 different paths to improvement, helps you identify a suitable path for your situation, and sets you on your way to success.

Knowing yourself and your portfolio of strengths and weaknesses is key. Study after study has found that self-awareness is a key factor associated with high performance and potential and an indicator of long-term career success. Individuals who are more self-aware are more likely to seek feedback in many forms, quicker to accept it, and more likely to act on it.

Research shows that having five to seven key strengths might be all you need to achieve success. But it's important to read the fine print. These strengths need to be in mission-critical areas that contribute to performance. Additionally, your weaknesses in mission-critical areas need to be dealt with so that they do not distract from your strengths. Finally, you can't have any fatal flaws— negative traits or behaviors that would stall your career.

Unfortunately, success is not as simple as self-awareness and a handful of mission-critical strengths. As you progress in your career, the requirements for success change. Strengths that contributed to your success in the past can have a negative effect later, especially if overused. On the flip side, weaknesses overlooked early in your career can catch up with you and create problems.

Given the dynamic nature of what's required for success, what are some routes that will get you to your destination? Research and experience suggest that there are many strategies for achieving your desired outcome. Depending on your skill level, the need, and the situation, the 14 paths in this book are all legitimate approaches to getting better results at work.

Let's say you received feedback from a direct report that you are not providing very clear directions about how the team should divide the workload. You have several possible paths that will help you improve: You could seek additional feedback to build more awareness of your need in this area. You could use another skill (like delegation or planning) to cover for, substitute for, or neutralize the negative effects of your lack of skill. You could work around the weakness by finding someone else to partner with you when it's time to distribute the workload and clearly communicate objectives. Of course, you could also choose to develop the skill directly, but a "fix-it" development plan is just one path of many.

Once you recognize the many paths you can take to improve, how do you determine which path to take? Here are a few factors to consider:

- *Awareness and acceptance.* If you are not aware of a weakness or a problem area, or if you do not accept the feedback that you are hearing, then you need to do some additional exploration. The Insight plan (p. 3) is the best way to build awareness and acceptance. (Another resource to explore is *FYI® for Insight*, a book designed to help you become more self-aware and build a realistic knowledge of your strengths and weaknesses.)

- *Willingness to take action.* It is one thing to be aware and accept the need to improve in an area; it's another to be willing to do something about it. To change your behavior. To invest in improving. Most plans in this book require you to be willing to act. There are two plans to choose from when, for whatever reason, you are not willing to take action: the Redeployment plan (p. 61) and the Capitulation plan (p. 65).

- *Skill building.* Some situations will require you to build the skill directly. Other times, it will be OK to keep the status quo on your skill level but supplement, complement, substitute, or address the need in some other fashion. Plans that build skill directly include the Development plan (p. 13), the Enhancement plan (p. 17), the Good to extraordinary plan (p. 21), and the Rerailment plan (p. 25).

- *Skill level.* The plan you choose will depend on whether you are weak, average, strong, or overusing the skill in question. It's also possible that you have not tried using the skill that you need. Find the plans that are appropriate for different skill levels by deciding whether you need to build the skill directly, find alternative paths, or demonstrate a skill you already possess. For help, turn to Figure 1 (p. 86) in the "How to select plans" section or refer to "Quick start" (p. iv).

- *Time frame.* Depending on the urgency of the situation, you may have a need that must be addressed within a week, or you may be able to take several months or years to improve. You can choose a path that fits your time frame. Or you can choose an interim path that gets you some immediate results and a long-term path that helps you improve over the long run. See Table 4 (p. 88) in the "How to select plans" section for more details. Each chapter indicates the path's relative time frame (shorter to longer):

- *Coaching support.* If you are working independently and you do not have a coach, mentor, or manager supporting you, there will be some plans that are easier for you to craft and implement on your own. Other plans require an expert coach, mentor, or boss to act as a partner, advise you, help you reflect, and keep you honest. Find out which plans require additional support by turning to Table 4 (p. 88) in the "How to select plans" section. Each chapter indicates whether the path can be pursued independently or whether it is most effective to partner with a coach:

If you do not have access to a coach, think of this book as your coach. When you see yourself in one of the examples or descriptions, see if the plan described might be a good fit for your need. Use this book along with the companion guide, *Paths to improvement: Navigating your way to success Coaching reference guide,* to create a plan that will help you address your need. To jump-start the process, turn to "Quick start" (p. iv).

Whether you are using the book for your own or someone else's benefit, knowing the possible paths to improvement is an important first step for career, performance, or development conversations. *Paths to improvement: Navigating your way to success* equips you with an interactive map offering multiple routes to get you to your destination—success.

| iii

Quick start

Where do I go when I need a plan?

About the authors

Robert W. Eichinger

Bob Eichinger has been working with managers and executives on leadership development for over 50 years. He is one of the founders and the former CEO of Lominger Limited, Inc. and co-creator of the Leadership Architect® Suite of management, executive, and organizational development tools. During his career, he has served as Vice Chairman of the Korn Ferry Institute, worked inside companies such as PepsiCo and Pillsbury, and as a consultant in Fortune 500 companies in the United States, Europe, Japan, Canada, and Australia. Dr. Eichinger lectures extensively on the topic of executive and management development and has served on the Board of the Human Resource Planning Society. He has worked as a coach with more than 1,000 managers and executives. Some of his books include *The Leadership Machine*, written with Mike Lombardo, *100 Things You Need to Know: Best People Practices for Managers & HR*, written with Mike Lombardo and Dave Ulrich, and *FYI® for Strategic Effectiveness*, written with Kim Ruyle and Dave Ulrich.

Michael M. Lombardo

Mike Lombardo has over 30 years experience in executive and management research and in executive coaching. He is one of the founders of Lominger Limited, Inc., publishers of the Leadership Architect® Suite. With Bob Eichinger, Mike has authored 40 products for the suite, including *The Leadership Machine*, *FYI® For Your Improvement*, the *Career Architect®*, *Choices Architect®*, and *VOICES®*. During his 15 years at the Center for Creative Leadership, Mike was a coauthor of *The Lessons of Experience*, which detailed which learnings from experience can teach the competencies needed to be successful. He also coauthored the research on executive derailment revealing how personal flaws and overdone strengths caused otherwise effective executives to get into career trouble, Benchmarks®, a 360º feedback instrument, and the Looking Glass® simulation. Mike has won five national awards for research on managerial and executive development.

Alex J. Stiber

Alex Stiber is an author and consultant who has worked extensively in the areas of business process change, organizational culture change, leadership and executive development, and organizational performance. He has designed and implemented training and development programs and facilitated change initiatives for many Fortune 500 organizations. Alex is coauthor of the book *Lost and Found: The Story of How One Man Discovered the Secrets of Leadership Where He Wasn't Even Looking*, as well as a contributor to other business books. He has also been a keynote speaker on the subjects of teams, leadership, talent management, and succession planning at national and international conferences; a guest lecturer on organizational culture in the graduate industrial management program at Carnegie Mellon University; and a graduate faculty member of the Duquesne University School of Leadership and Professional Advancement, specializing in Decision Making and Problem Solving for leaders. Alex has an MA in creative writing, and published over 40 poems and short stories in international journals before turning his focus to business.

J. Evelyn Orr

Evelyn Orr is an Intellectual Property Development Consultant for Korn Ferry Leadership and Talent Consulting. She is coauthor of the Lominger publication *FYI® for Insight: The 21 Leadership Characteristics for Success and the 5 That Get You Fired* and has many years of experience in talent management, including competency modeling, interviewing and selection, engagement, leadership development, team development, and succession planning. She has held leadership positions in a large retail organization and served as a consultant with over a dozen Fortune 500 companies from a variety of industries. Evelyn is coauthor of several papers and articles, including *Setting the Stage for Success: Building the Leadership Skills That Matter*, *Best Practices in Developing and Implementing Competency Models*, *Fundamentals of Competency Development,* and *Illuminating Blind Spots and Hidden Strengths*.

Acknowledgments

We would like to express our gratitude to a number of people who contributed ideas and assistance in the preparation of this book.

Kevin Mlodzik did an outstanding job completing a thorough literature review as well as conducting a research study to ensure we were current and research-based in our recommendations.

Kim Ruyle, Ken De Meuse, George Hallenbeck, and Vicki Swisher served as thought partners and reviewers. They made great suggestions which improved the book.

Many consultants, associates, and coaches were involved in providing feedback and ideas that enhanced the book. A special thanks to Karen Dorece for her contribution.

As always, we are in awe of our amazing production team—Lesley Kurke, Doug Lodermeier Sr., Paul Montei, and Bonnie Parks—all of whom did an excellent job of proofing, editing, design, layout, and production.

We appreciate the contributions of all.

Deeper exploration

1	**Insight plan**
2	**Exposure plan**

Knowing yourself, your unique portfolio of strengths and weaknesses, is the first step toward improving. You can't get to where you want to go if you don't know your starting point. Not knowing where you stand could be due to lack of self-awareness, confusing or inconsistent feedback, or lack of experience using specific skills. On the other hand, you may think you have a clear understanding of your skills but your perception is off compared to other people's perceptions of you. All of the above represent opportunities to explore more deeply and develop a more accurate and complete picture of your current state.

1 Insight plan

Increase self-awareness and better understand yourself.

What is the Insight plan?

The Insight plan will help you develop a greater self-awareness of your portfolio strengths and weaknesses. The plan could involve self-reflection or asking bosses, colleagues, or others for more feedback. Whatever it is, it should help you recognize and eliminate potential blind spots—areas where you think you are more skilled than other people think you are. The Insight plan can also shed light on potential derailers—issues that could cause so much trouble for you that they obscure your portfolio of strengths. The goal is to achieve a more accurate awareness of yourself so you can take steps to reach your potential. You can't get somewhere else until you know where you are now.

When do I use this plan?

The Insight plan is appropriate in a number of situations:

- *You do not understand what is inhibiting your performance.* Something is amiss. You are unable to make the impact or get the results you and others expect. You are tempted to blame the situation, find fault in others, or shrug your shoulders and leave it a mystery. But you know those are not fruitful options. On the other hand, seeking feedback about your skills and behaviors requires courage. The Insight plan can provide the structure and direction to gather and analyze feedback in a supportive environment.

- *You do not understand the feedback you're getting.* Sometimes it's hard to make sense of the feedback because it's intermittent and inconsistent. It's possible, for example, that your peers view you as compassionate, but your direct reports don't. Or your boss thinks you are a strong problem solver, but your peers think you have a weakness there. More often than not, these types of scenarios are a result of behavior on your part that is context- or situation-dependent. In fact, you may behave differently with people in the same constituency—for example, being viewed as approachable by two direct reports but not by a third. Just because the feedback is inconsistent or you don't understand the problem doesn't mean there isn't a problem.

The way to move ahead in these situations is to get additional sources of credible feedback.

- *You do not agree that a skill deficit is as bad as others are saying, and you're starting to get defensive.* Maybe you're in denial about a weakness or unable to accept that your weakness is really such a big problem. Stark disagreement with consistent feedback from others usually means that you do not know yourself very well. Your goal is to narrow the gap between your own and others' perceptions. Gaining additional insight and building self-awareness can help you avoid trouble. Self-aware leaders are more likely to be higher performers and have greater long-term career success.

- *You have tried to work on the issue, but others are still not seeing improvement.* Accepting feedback is one thing. Understanding the underlying cause is the next crucial element to creating a successful improvement plan. For example, you could go home and during dinner say to your spouse, "You know, a curious thing happened today at work. Many of the raters on my 360° feedback said that I'm not improving at listening. What do you think?" To which your spouse answers, "I'll be glad to tell you, but only if you promise not to interrupt me again!" In this case, understanding why you don't listen can be the key to changing the underlying beliefs and assumptions that drive your behavior.

How do I use this plan?

Depending on your situation and your openness to self-discovery and insight, the application of the Insight plan may range from the simple to the more radical and in-depth.

Sometimes self-reflection can increase insight or self-knowledge, but often you will need feedback—an outside perspective.

- If you get inconsistent feedback and have trouble making sense of it, you will need to collect additional, more objective feedback from a coach, a mentor, or some type of skills inventory or personality assessment.

- If you don't agree with the feedback you have been given, get additional sources of credible feedback from mentors, trusted associates, past bosses, or even your spouse. Also consider some additional assessment and calibration.

- Watch out for defensiveness and resistance. Be willing to accept that you are wrong. The acceptance process can require a skilled coach to build accurate awareness of the issues.

At some point, you may have deeper issues that are causing noise at work or at home that you are not willing to acknowledge or address. In order to resolve these more serious situations, you will need to rely on experts such as an assessment specialist, a diagnostic coach, a counselor, or an employee assistance program resource.

Self-knowledge is one of the most valuable skills you can develop since it is a foundation for so many others. When in doubt, pursue additional opportunities for insight. And remember this caution: lack of self-awareness and insight is a ticking bomb. There are many ways in which you can learn more about yourself—many sources of feedback—your boss, peers, significant other, friends, even enemies. Build self-knowledge by pursuing additional opportunities for insight. If you are a person who wants to take time to self-reflect and understand potential blind spots, you'll find tools like the *FYI® for Insight* book and online self-awareness assessment to be great places to start. Visit our *FYI® for Insight* web site at http://Insight.lominger.com.

Example

Sanjay thinks he's a whiz at sizing people up. "I can tell the winners from the losers as soon as I meet them," he has bragged more than once. Based on his belief in his infallible people instincts and intuition, Sanjay assigns people to well-defined areas of responsibility and then closely monitors their performance.

And Sanjay gets pretty good confirmation of his faith in his judgment. When Sanjay thinks someone is a "low burner," he puts the person in roles where they aren't going to be challenged. Then, when the person doesn't achieve great things, shows little motivation, and gets disgruntled, Sanjay says, "See, I told you."

Sanjay has been a strong individual contributor and has a wealth of technical knowledge as well as other strengths his organization prizes. As Sanjay transitions to management, it will be important for him to skillfully assess and deploy people. Unfortunately, Sanjay's inordinate faith in his own judgment about people creates some bad self-fulfilling prophecies.

A coach meets with Sanjay to review feedback from direct reports alleging that he is controlling, arrogant, and not empowering. Sanjay has heard it all before and rejected it outright. The coach presents some additional data pointing out how unpredictable performance and higher-than-average turnover are emerging problems in Sanjay's group. This gets Sanjay's attention. He's willing to acknowledge that there is a problem. Getting acceptance of the precise problem and diagnosing the root cause will help Sanjay get the insight he needs in order to avoid the imminent derailment others see in his future.

Paths to improvement plan

Paths to improvement plan

Name: *Sanjay*   Date to be completed by: *Week of January 15*

1 What is the GAP?

Sizing up people
I would like to select and deploy people effectively. I thought that I was good at this, but it seems like my track record is questionable. From the results I'm seeing, it appears that I am overconfident in my ability to assess talent. This is a critical skill for me to get right.

2 What is the GOAL?

I want to be able to read people accurately, diagnose strengths, weaknesses, and potential. I want to hire the best people so that I can have the best team, but first I need to figure out what is going wrong and why.

3 How will I get there? What PATH will I take?

Deeper exploration
☒ Insight plan
☐ Exposure plan

Direct skill building
☐ Development plan
☐ Enhancement plan
☐ Good to extraordinary plan
☐ Rerailment plan

Alternative paths
☐ Substitution plan
☐ Workaround plan
☐ Compensation plan

Demonstrating skill
☐ Marketing plan
☐ Skill transfer plan
☐ Confidence building plan

Accepting the consequences
☐ Redeployment plan
☐ Capitulation plan

4 What is my PLAN? What are my action steps?

As a substitute, the only skill that would be a good crutch for me to lean on while I work out this issue is Managing and measuring work. I can clearly assign responsibility and set clear objectives for my team. I will provide more regular feedback on progress so that they are set up for success as much as possible.

I will partner with my coach to observe my thought process and decision-making process so that we can better understand the root cause of my issue with Sizing up people. I will also seek feedback from others. Once we diagnose why I'm failing at this, I will create a Development plan.

5 What is the TIME LINE?

I'd like to get at the root causes within the next 2 months.

2 Exposure plan

Try out an untested skill to see where you stand.

> **“**One of the reasons people stop learning is
> that they become less and less willing to risk failure.**”**
>
> John W. Gardner – Former U.S. Secretary of Health, Education, and Welfare

What is the Exposure plan?

The Exposure plan will help you gain knowledge and experience in areas which are new and untested for you. It pairs an important but untested skill with an assignment that requires you to give it a try. Until you are exposed to certain experiences and situations that require a particular skill, your skill level and potential ability in that skill remain a mystery. This plan removes some of the mystery and gives you a sense of your existing or potential ability in an untested area.

When do I use this plan?

- *You have not had the opportunity to try out a skill in your current or past jobs.* Sometimes you will get feedback and see a low rating and respond, "Well, of course no one thinks I'm any good at that—I've never had a chance to try it." What do you do if you simply haven't tried it, here or elsewhere? Untested areas are often skills (like negotiating or strategy) that previous jobs didn't call on you to do. If it's really a matter of your not having had a chance to do it and show it, then the Exposure plan is the appropriate approach. Find an opportunity to put the "untested" skill to the test.

Say, for instance, that people who assessed you seemed to think you're not good at team building. And they also think that team building is important in your organization because there's so much attention given to it by senior leaders. So, if team building is really important to your career, find an opportunity to build a team; take on a project that requires you to do that. You may think you're good at it; others may suppose that you're good at it. What you need is real data so that you can assess where you are. If you get an opportunity to engage in team building and do poorly, you'll know, based on your career plans, whether that's something to start addressing.

How do I use this plan?

It's essential to assess how important the untested skill is for your current job and how important it will be for your continued career. If you're perceived as unskilled at something and it is relatively low on importance, addressing it probably isn't a high priority. If, however, people say it is important or will be important, and also rate you low, then you should do something about it.

Keep in mind, since you have never used the skill before, the most likely outcome is that you will be somewhere between low and average. Until you have had some exposure and practice, it's not likely you would start off as outstanding. Therefore, make sure you are realistic in your expectations. Seek both challenge and support when you test yourself.

Example

Ang landed a great entry-level procurement job with a major medical device company. Vendor management isn't a career Ang would have aspired to in college, mostly because he didn't know enough about how companies function. But now, the work seems interesting enough—writing requests for proposals, evaluating responses, arranging demonstrations, negotiating the terms of the agreement.

During one of Ang's touchbase meetings with his manager, she expressed reservation in Ang's ability to negotiate the best deal. "I'm going to put Rachel on point for negotiation on this project; I just don't think you've got what it takes," she informed Ang. Ang found it difficult to argue. After searching his mind for examples of his negotiation ability, he couldn't come up with a single one. He hadn't even negotiated the sale price for his car—his dad had taken care of that.

Disappointed and a little less engaged, Ang spent the next few weeks in a support role backing up Rachel on the project. When quarterly development conversations came around, however, Ang had worked up the motivation and nerve to ask for an opportunity to try it on his own—negotiate an actual contract. Ang had worked out a persuasive argument for every possible objection, and he was prepared to be direct as well as diplomatic about his proposition.

Fortunately, Ang's approach worked. His boss agreed, saying, "There's been some discussion about changing the vendor that does background checks for recruiting. It's not a huge amount of money at stake, but the company is trying to cut back and every bit counts. You can take the lead on that and we'll see how you fare."

| 9

Paths to improvement plan

Paths to improvement plan

Name: *Ang*   Date to be completed by: *September end of month*

1 What is the **GAP?**

Negotiating
I haven't ever really had to negotiate. I don't know whether I'll be able to win concessions while keeping the relationship positive. I know I'll have to build trust. And I know there's a method to it. That's what I want to learn.

2 What is the **GOAL?**

If I want to continue in vendor management and get promoted to the next level, it's really important for me to learn how to negotiate effective contracts. My goal is to get the best deal for our company that leaves the vendor feeling like they want to continue to do business with us.

3 How will I get there? What **PATH** will I take?

Deeper exploration
☐ Insight plan
☒ Exposure plan

Direct skill building
☐ Development plan
☐ Enhancement plan
☐ Good to extraordinary plan
☐ Rerailment plan

Alternative paths
☐ Substitution plan
☐ Workaround plan
☐ Compensation plan

Demonstrating skill
☐ Marketing plan
☐ Skill transfer plan
☐ Confidence building plan

Accepting the consequences
☐ Redeployment plan
☐ Capitulation plan

4 What is my **PLAN?** What are my action steps?

I know that I will need to call upon some other skills while I get my negotiating skills up to speed. I'll focus on staying composed and using my listening skills as well as my motivating skills—I'm good at tapping into what's important to other people and seeing things from their perspectives.

I'm taking the lead on the background check vendor project—all phases, including negotiating the final contract with the selected vendor.

Get feedback from my boss throughout the project.

5 What is the **TIME LINE?**

The project I'll work on is starting in two weeks and is due to wrap up at the end of September.

Direct skill building

3 Development plan

4 Enhancement plan

5 Good to extraordinary plan

6 Rerailment plan

The key ingredients required for building skill in any area are motivation, perseverance, and humility. Identify the skills that are most essential for success in your current job or dream job—your career goals and the needs of the organization intersect here. While it may not be realistic to take a weakness and convert it into a towering strength, it is possible to move the needle. Average skills or strengths can also benefit from direct skill building, or development. Several factors can increase your chances of success. Gather feedback. Seek out developmental experiences. Be willing to learn and change based on what you observe and experience. Find sources of support such as a coach, mentor, peer advisor, or an advocate to help you stay motivated and on track.

3 Development plan

Work on a weakness.

> *" It is the capacity to develop and improve their skills that distinguishes leaders from followers. "*
>
> Warren Bennis – American scholar and author

What is the Development plan?

The Development plan will help you build skill in an area of weakness. This plan, sometimes called an individual development plan, or IDP, is the ubiquitous plan we've all used or tried to use. When you adopt this plan, you're deciding that you're going to fix one or more weaknesses. Most successful leaders have five to seven towering strengths, but importantly, they also lack glaring weaknesses in mission-critical areas.

When do I use this plan?

The Development plan is most effective in the following circumstances:

- *You are aware of your weakness and you want to build skill in a mission-critical area.* When we talk about "fixing" a weakness, we're not suggesting that your goal should be to move it from a weakness to a strength (arguably an unrealistic goal), but rather to reduce the noise and move it to a level of acceptable performance.

- *You accept your weakness.* If you haven't accepted a weakness that is limiting your success, a Development plan will not help you. If you are still in denial, rationalizing, confused, or defensive about having this weakness, start with an Insight plan and get some additional feedback and counsel.

- *You are motivated to do something about your weakness.* Without the drive, urgency, and energy to do something about a weakness, writing a Development plan will not help you. Developing a weakness is one of the hardest things to do, and most Development plans fail because people don't follow through.

How do I use this plan?

First, determine your need. Make sure you determine what your real need is. Many times you may have to select a few skills that together equal your actual need. Try to find the true underlying need, not just what's showing up on the surface. If you think you have a problem getting results, ask yourself why. Maybe the real problem is lack of composure or courage, or delegating. Perhaps you only have trouble with results when one of these is demanded.

Developmental strategies to build skill are straightforward. In all cases, you attack the need directly. For the Development plan, you are weak in an important area and you'd like to get better—neutralize the weakness by at least becoming average.

Then, take action. When you have identified a need, follow recommendations that sprouted from years of research on developing skills:

- *See the target.* If you want to develop a skill, you need to envision the ideal. Think of someone who is widely considered to be the best at what you want to work on. Picture that person in meetings. You note the things that person does. Develop a model of what it looks like to be skilled and establish that as your reference point.

- *See yourself in comparison to the target.* Compare your current skill level to the ideal. What is the distance between you and your model? What do they do that you don't do? If you aren't sure, whom could you ask for feedback?

- *See the reason to change.* You need motivation to improve—you must link your behavior or your need to improve to consequences and clearly appreciate how improving in a particular area would make you more effective in your overall performance. So you ask yourself, "What's this deficit costing me, and am I really committed to changing and improving in this area?" If your honest answer is "I don't care," or "I'm not sure," then don't bother—you will only be going through the motions.

- *Find people, courses, and ideas that help you develop your skill.* Assuming you've contemplated the change and decided it's important, you need to figure out how you're going to improve. What are your options? You could go to a training course in effective listening—plenty of those around. Or you could read a good book on the subject. Another helpful approach is to identify role models—learn from their example and ask for their feedback when they observe you.

- *Seek on-the-job experiences that demand and test your skill.* The number one developer of competence by far is stretching, challenging jobs. Feedback, courses, and role models are great, but jobs are where you really develop and exercise significant and varied skills. You have to stretch in uncomfortable areas. A challenging job or assignment requires you to work on your downsides more vigorously because you either perform or fail. Real development happens when it's not practice but it's the real thing and the stakes are high. Think back to your greatest challenges and hardships— those can be the experiences that helped you grow the most. While it's possible to actively seek out those challenges, sometimes you happen upon them—it's good to be ready by keeping your development goals in mind.

- *Reflect and reinforce your new skill.* Reflect on what you've done, make sense of it. Keep a journal. Develop guidelines, dos and don'ts, and rules of thumb for yourself that you can use to guide your behavior so that it becomes increasingly natural to you. If you are one of the many who are drafting and implementing annual Development plans, you'll find a tool like *FYI® For Your Improvement* 5th Edition to be a great starting point.

Example

Sanjay had previously executed an Insight plan (see page 3). Sanjay had a blind spot in assessing and deploying talent—he was not able to accurately size up a person's strengths and weaknesses and match the person to the right assignments. Now that Sanjay knows his blind spot, it is no longer a blind spot. It's a weakness. And he knows he needs to improve in order to progress in his career.

The Insight plan helped Sanjay identify some root causes for his failure in this area. For one, he was jumping to conclusions too quickly. He would grab hold of a little data—from a resume or a reference or a first impression—and extrapolate that into what he thought was a robust evaluation. Instead, it was subjective and incomplete. And, on a related note, Sanjay noticed his tendency to assume that if someone was a stellar performer in one area, it was a foregone conclusion that they would excel in unrelated areas as well. His coach told Sanjay that decision biases like these are quite common.

Armed with this new information, Sanjay is ready to get down to business and get better at Sizing up people.

Paths to improvement plan

Paths to improvement plan

Name: *Sanjay*   Date to be completed by: *September*

1 What is the **GAP?**

Sizing up people
I don't evaluate the strengths and weaknesses of others well. And I have trouble incorporating additional data after my initial appraisal.

2 What is the **GOAL?**

I want to be able to read people accurately, diagnose strengths, weaknesses, and potential. I want to hire the best people and make sure that I'm setting everyone up for success by matching their skill sets to the right roles.

3 How will I get there? What **PATH** will I take?

Deeper exploration
☐ Insight plan
☐ Exposure plan

Direct skill building
☒ Development plan
☐ Enhancement plan
☐ Good to extraordinary plan
☐ Rerailment plan

Alternative paths
☐ Substitution plan
☐ Workaround plan
☐ Compensation plan

Demonstrating skill
☐ Marketing plan
☐ Skill transfer plan
☐ Confidence building plan

Accepting the consequences
☐ Redeployment plan
☐ Capitulation plan

4 What is my **PLAN?** What are my action steps?

I will continue my focus on Managing and measuring work by clearly assigning responsibility and setting clear objectives for my team. I will continue to provide more regular feedback on progress so that they are set up for success as much as possible.

Take the HR course on interviewing and selection that's being offered so I better understand the criteria and tools for evaluating candidates.

One of my peers is known for being a "talent magnet" and producing some of the best newly promoted managers and leaders from her group. I'll ask her to be an interviewer so we can compare notes and I can learn from her observations.

I still have an open requisition that needs to be filled quickly. I will use this on-the-job experience to make sure I slow down, take in additional data points, and make sure that I'm checking my assumptions about a candidate's strengths and weaknesses.

5 What is the **TIME LINE?**

Our team has to deliver on a major initiative in 9 months. I would like to see everyone be individually and collectively successful on that project.

4 Enhancement plan

Move a mission-critical skill from average to a strength.

> *"That's the news from Lake Woebegon, where all the women are strong, all the men are good-looking, and all the children are above average."*

Garrison Keillor – American author, storyteller, and radio personality

What is the Enhancement plan?

The Enhancement plan will help you focus on moving from average to strong in a mission-critical area. It's the appropriate plan when you're doing OK on a mission-critical competency, but being better than OK would be a good investment.

When do I use this plan?

Use the Enhancement plan when:

- *You do not hesitate to admit that you are average at a mission-critical skill.* When you're average in a skill and you know it, learning on the job, learning from others, and learning from courses will be more effective in your average areas than in your areas of weakness. Because you are at least competent in an area, you're less likely to be as defensive about it, less likely to reject feedback on that area, and less likely to resist efforts to help you improve—all obstacles to change. Because you are not resisting, it will be easier to improve.

- *You want to see a significant payoff for the effort you're investing in your development.* Focusing on improving in areas where you are already average can result in a big payoff. Moving from average to better than average has a much higher success rate than trying to move a weakness to average. You already have a head start. You are not working from a deficit. Also, you have more room to show improvement than if you were working on moving a strength to a towering strength. Often, your improvement can be measured in real terms with key business metrics such as increased sales or higher margins.

How do I use this plan?

Imagine you have always thought of yourself as an adequate problem solver— maybe not the one everybody turns to when they've got a really complex problem to solve, but at least someone who can be counted on to contribute to finding a solution.

Apparently, others agree with you: your phone's not ringing off the hook, but no one is avoiding you either. You have decided that your organization and the quickly changing and ever-more-complex environment require you to become a better, stronger problem solver. If you had been terrible at it, there would be less hope. But, even without trying to become good, you've always been adequate. Here is an area where your odds are good.

You probably have good judgment and other qualities that play into problem solving, like being analytical. So, what do you do now? For one thing, you can read a great book on problem solving and systems thinking, like Dietrich Dörner's *The Logic of Failure*. Interview someone who is thought of as a great problem solver to find out what that person does, how they do it, and how they learned it. Finally, get involved in spearheading a major problem-solving effort.

You might ask why we distinguish this type of plan under its own heading since it seems to be only an application of the Development plan (see page 13) and in all other key respects has the structure of one. The reason is simple: "development" plans, as they have been applied, have generally been thought of as a remedy for weakness, a fix for what's broken. But since we know that you'll get more return on your investment by moving average performance to good performance, and, in turn, good performance to superior performance (see the Good to extraordinary plan, page 21), the concept of enhancement is more than a semantic distinction.

Example

As Ang worked through an Exposure plan (see page 7) to test his skill in negotiation, he and his manager realized that he's actually OK at it. Turns out, that course in negotiation strategies he took in college had some useful tips and tricks that Ang was able to apply. The contract negotiations for the company's background check vendor went very smoothly. Ang was able to get some added perks by carefully structuring the agreement and payment schedule.

Ang's manager knows that Negotiating is one of the harder skills to develop and a rare skill among entry-level employees. In her development coaching conversation with Ang, she strongly recommended that he consider converting it into a strength. Ang is eager to differentiate himself in this mission-critical area and agreed to create an Enhancement plan.

Paths to improvement plan

Paths to improvement plan

Name: *Ang*   Date to be completed by: *August*

1 What is the **GAP?**	*Negotiating* *Going from average to strong in Negotiating would really distinguish me from my peers and position me to grow my career in vendor management.*
2 What is the **GOAL?**	*My goal is to skillfully win concessions without damaging relationships and to be both assertive and diplomatic.*

3 How will I get there? What **PATH** will I take?

Deeper exploration	Alternative paths	Accepting the consequences
☐ Insight plan	☐ Substitution plan	
☐ Exposure plan	☐ Workaround plan	☐ Redeployment plan
	☐ Compensation plan	☐ Capitulation plan
Direct skill building	**Demonstrating skill**	
☐ Development plan	☐ Marketing plan	
☒ Enhancement plan	☐ Skill transfer plan	
☐ Good to extraordinary plan	☐ Confidence building plan	
☐ Rerailment plan		

4 What is my **PLAN?** What are my action steps?

I will continue to leverage Listening and Motivating others as well as Composure.

I'm going to dig up my notes from that great negotiation course I took in college. I think there are a lot of principles and strategies that will be helpful for me to keep in mind.

There are a couple of executives who have negotiated big strategic deals for our company. I'm going to invite each of them to lunch to ask questions and learn from their experiences. Maybe one of them will agree to be my mentor.

My boss is pairing me with a director in our department on a significant upcoming project—renegotiating the contract with one of our key suppliers. I will learn so much from watching Sara in action and working with her on this. I also get to take the lead on food service and printer/copier services—nothing super risky, but a challenging enough next step that will help me figure out how to balance interpersonal skills with business priorities.

5 What is the **TIME LINE?**

I will focus on this for most of the next year. This is a tough skill to develop, so I want to give myself adequate time. I will have regular check-ins with my manager to get ongoing feedback.

|

5 Good to extraordinary plan

Move a strength to outstanding.

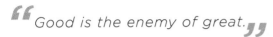 *Good is the enemy of great.*

James C. Collins III – American business consultant and author

What is the Good to extraordinary plan?

The Good to extraordinary plan will help you build a strength into a towering strength. You may be near the top, but you haven't reached the top yet. It's the equivalent of being a thousand feet short of the summit at Everest. Many people make it that far, but you want to be among the elite who have made it to the top. This plan raises your performance in a mission-critical area from talented to one of the best that people have seen. It involves a commitment to continuous improvement that is driven by an organizational and personal vision of excellence.

When do I use this plan?

- *You want to differentiate yourself as the best in this area.* You are ready to develop a deeper expertise and be the best. You are enthusiastic and motivated to learn from the best, even though you can hold your own in this area. You are not willing to settle for "good enough."

- *You have career ambition and you want to be a successful leader and top executive.* When you consider all of the skills that are mission critical to your current or future role, you need to be outstanding in several and not have any glaring weaknesses in the others. The most successful executives have five to seven towering strengths in the top 10% skill level compared to all other leaders' skill levels.

How do I use this plan?

You need some important information, a skilled coach, and the right attitude for this plan to work.

- *You need to know which skills matter most.* You don't have to guess which skills matter most. Decades of research on leadership has done that work for you. We know the leadership skills that matter most. This would be a good time to review *FYI® For Your Improvement* 5th Edition or

FYI® for Insight—two books that catalogue a library of leadership skills. Of course, the skills you prioritize will depend on your level, your industry, your function, and your job description. Your company may already have a competency model in place that articulates what's most important for success. Work with your manager or coach to define the mission-critical competencies that are most relevant to success in your role and for the future.

- *You need feedback to help determine where you stand on the mission-critical skills that contribute to success.* You can get feedback by participating in a multi-rater 360° assessment, by asking your manager to informally rate you on a set of skills, or by making it a practice to ask for feedback from others on a regular basis. Once you have a good sense of your skill level in mission-critical areas, you can choose a strength and work to convert it to a towering strength.

- *You need an outstanding skills coach.* This will not be easy because very few coaches will qualify. Try to find a coach who is an expert and ranks in the top 1% of the skill you are working on. Additionally, it is important for this person to be an expert coach who is able to provide insight and feedback, and who will patiently work with you to find the final critical tweaks that will move you from talented to one of the best.

- *You need patience and humility.* You are already very talented in the skill, so you have probably been complimented and rewarded for your ability in this area for many years. However, if you want to be the best, you will need to approach this plan with a learner's mentality. Humility and patience will be assets for you here. Humility will help you be receptive to feedback and recognize opportunities for improvement. Patience will give you the endurance and persistence required to perfect the adjustments that will propel you to the top.

Example

Aubrey, a VP in a small service company, is on the fast track. She's young, likable, ambitious, and an avid learner. She has her sights set on nothing less than being president of the company.

The CEO recently enlisted the help of an external consultant to coach Aubrey and to help her create a challenging improvement plan for the coming year.

The coach learned from Aubrey's 360° feedback, as well as from interviews with the CEO, her peers, and her direct reports, that Aubrey is generally seen as well balanced and strong in all of the mission-critical competencies. All key competencies were rated at least skilled/OK or above. Learning on the fly was her highest-rated item by all groups.

Knowing that successful executives have several towering strengths and no glaring weaknesses, the coach wanted to focus on building some of Aubrey's strengths into extraordinary strengths. He focused on the skills that were rated essential in importance and skills where Aubrey was rated talented or above.

The options included:

- Business acumen
- Decision quality
- Priority setting
- *Managing* vision and purpose
- Strategic agility
- Comfort around higher management
- *Dealing with* ambiguity
- Problem solving

After some discussion, Aubrey and her coach decided that she should focus on *Managing* vision and purpose—a mission-critical strength for executives that is in short supply.

Paths to improvement plan

Paths to improvement plan

Name: *Aubrey*   Date to be completed by: *March*

1 What is the GAP?

Managing vision and purpose
The leaders I most admire are ones who are really great at communicating vision, purpose, and strategy. I would like to move the needle on Managing vision and purpose so that it's one of my towering strengths.

2 What is the GOAL?

My goal is not to focus on inspiring speeches or broad communication strategies—I really want to focus on customizing the message and the vision for different individuals and constituencies.

3 How will I get there? What PATH will I take?

Deeper exploration
- ☐ Insight plan
- ☐ Exposure plan

Direct skill building
- ☐ Development plan
- ☐ Enhancement plan
- ☒ Good to extraordinary plan
- ☐ Rerailment plan

Alternative paths
- ☐ Substitution plan
- ☐ Workaround plan
- ☐ Compensation plan

Demonstrating skill
- ☐ Marketing plan
- ☐ Skill transfer plan
- ☐ Confidence building plan

Accepting the consequences
- ☐ Redeployment plan
- ☐ Capitulation plan

4 What is my PLAN? What are my action steps?

I've signed up for a six-week executive education course at a prestigious business school. This should give me additional grounding in the principles of communicating vision and purpose.

Our CEO has connections with a few executives in other companies who are amazing at articulating the vision and motivating people during times of change. I'm going to meet with them to learn how they handled some challenging situations and managed to stay optimistic. I will make an effort to communicate our vision to people with different interests.

The company is embarking on a major change initiative that will impact everyone—from field employees, to corporate functions, vendors, and customers. I am going to work on building relationships and understanding the perspectives of many stakeholders. I want to hone how I tailor the message and motivate diverse stakeholder groups and individuals.

5 What is the TIME LINE?

Because Managing vision and purpose is moderately difficult to develop, I'm going to give myself 6-9 months to see some marked improvement.

6 Rerailment plan

Get performance back on track after a serious stumble.

❝Failures in life are often preceded by warning signs that we don't pick up on, either because they´re not loud enough or we´re not paying attention... When the little warnings fail to do their job, the universe simply bumps up its campaign to get you back on track.❞

Kay Cassidy – American author

What is the Rerailment plan?

The Rerailment plan helps you identify career derailers or stallers that are causing a serious problem and helps you address them by building self-awareness. Instead of being focused on a lack of skill, the focus of the Rerailment plan is on the presence of a problem (sometimes referred to as a *staller* or a *staller and stopper* because it can stall or stop your career very quickly). A Rerailment plan is serious and takes concentrated effort as well as partnership with a skilled coach.

When do I use this plan?

- *You have received feedback that you likely have a serious problem in an area that could severely disrupt or limit your career.* That is, you've received feedback that you are in jeopardy on one or more of the 19 career stallers and stoppers (also referred to as derailers in the research from the Center for Creative Leadership). You're going around a curve, the guardrail isn't adequate, the tracks are slick, and your wheels aren't securely tightened. Time to heed the warnings!

- *You have moved up the ladder very quickly and the combination of overused strengths and weaknesses is causing trouble for you.* If you are on the fast track, you probably got where you are by being highly proficient in your areas of expertise, by taking charge, solving problems, and getting results. But with that profile often comes some areas of vulnerability, like excessive independence, inadequate listening, lack of patience, inflexibility. In too many cases, weaknesses pair with overused strengths and—whoops!—you're off the performance or career track.

- *You have been or are about to be fired from your job or knocked off your projected career track.* Maybe you did not see or heed early warning signs and now you are suffering the consequences. While you are tempted to blame the situation, the organization, or the person who took your place, deep down you suspect that your leadership behaviors and abilities may have had something to do with this negative result.

How do I use this plan?

If you haven't already, find a skilled coach. When you are in danger of derailing, skilled coaching is typically required to help you increase self-awareness, neutralize the noise, and then raise your skill levels associated with the positive alternatives to the problem behavior.

Heed the warning signals. Warnings could be direct like critical feedback and poor performance ratings, or warnings could be indirect like being excluded from key conversations and not being sought out for your expertise. Heeding the warnings is a matter of becoming aware that you have a potential problem and accepting it. Let's say you are generally viewed as arrogant. To work on this problem, you must hear the feedback and accept the legitimacy of other people's perspectives, understand the consequences of not dealing with it, and determine that you're going to do something about it.

In confronting stallers and stoppers, it is helpful to identify the corresponding positive leadership skills that you can use or build in order to alleviate the problem. For example, if Overmanaging your direct reports is a problem, ramping up your ability in Delegation and Developing direct reports and others can help. Also, determine whether it is an overused strength that has caused the staller to flare up. For example, Intellectual horsepower gone into overdrive is often an underlying cause for being perceived as Arrogant.

As always, remember the 70:20:10 principle: 70% on-the-job learning through activities and assignments; 20% through people and assessment; 10% through courseware and readings of books like *FYI® For Your Improvement* 5th Edition, which provides a list of typical causes, identifies associated competency factors and clusters, and discusses remedies.

Example

Mary worked hard for her promotion to senior director. Now, she wants to prove she can deliver. She is skeptical that the team she inherited will be able to contribute the quality, timely work products she expects. Because Mary does not trust her team, she is beginning to demonstrate some troubling behaviors. She does not leverage her team's capabilities. And when she does delegate work, she meddles.

In Mary's mind, she reasons that she didn't rely on anyone else to get where she is today, so why should she start now? She firmly believes that she can power through and deliver the work of her entire team without much contribution from others. Her focus is on short-term results. Mary does not have the patience required to build teams, inspire others, and cultivate talent. She lacks a strategic perspective about people.

The result is that, unlike some of Mary's peers who have a reputation for being talent magnets or talent factories, Mary is viewed as talent repellant. No one wants to work for her. Those who do work for her do not grow or develop. Morale is suffering and business results are sagging.

Mary needs to begin empowering her team and do less of the work herself in order to keep her career from faltering.

Paths to improvement plan

Paths to improvement plan

Name: _Mary_   Date to be completed by: _March_

1 What is the GAP?

Overmanaging
I am seen as overmanaging my team. And, that appears to be true. Now that I understand that I have been doing too much myself and not developing my team, I know I need to fix this.

2 What is the GOAL?

I want to stop overmanaging so that I can focus on the right priorities. I want to give my people the chance to develop new skills. I will ensure that my people are qualified and motivated to do the work.

3 How will I get there? What PATH will I take?

Deeper exploration
☐ Insight plan
☐ Exposure plan

Direct skill building
☐ Development plan
☐ Enhancement plan
☐ Good to extraordinary plan
☒ Rerailment plan

Alternative paths
☐ Substitution plan
☐ Workaround plan
☐ Compensation plan

Demonstrating skill
☐ Marketing plan
☐ Skill transfer plan
☐ Confidence building plan

Accepting the consequences
☐ Redeployment plan
☐ Capitulation plan

4 What is my PLAN? What are my action steps?

I am going to work on coaching and mentoring my team members in areas where they show potential and interest. Two projects are starting up which will require project leads. I will identify and work with those individuals to enable them to take on more and more responsibility.

A couple of my peers are known for their ability to develop and empower others. I am going to build peer mentoring relationships with them. This will help me understand what they do well and give me a chance to troubleshoot and bounce ideas off them.

I will use my training and development budget. The courses won't be for me as much as for my team. I am going to strategically allocate training dollars for individuals who can come back from courses and contribute even more.

5 What is the TIME LINE?

After relying on myself for so long, I think this needs to be a somewhat gradual transition because I need to set my team up for success.

Alternative paths

7 Substitution plan

8 Workaround plan

9 Compensation plan

You don't have to be good at everything. Developing in all areas is unlikely. Development requires a lot of time, effort, and motivation. Also, some skills are more difficult to develop than others. Fortunately, development is not the only way to improve. If direct skill development seems unlikely, use other indirect strategies. Substitute something else you're good at for the lack of skill. Work around the need by relying on other people or trading tasks, or find work that better fits your skill profile. Moderate overused strengths by using compensator skills. Using alternative paths such as substitutes, workarounds, or compensators are a resourceful and creative way to improve at work.

7 Substitution plan

Use something else you're good at
to get the same thing done.

"She had a pretty gift for quotation, which is a serviceable substitute for wit."

William Somerset Maugham – English playwright and novelist

What is the Substitution plan?

The Substitution plan will help you get results by applying your strengths in place of a weakness. That is, you are substituting skills you are already good at to cover for or neutralize the negative effects of a weakness.

When do I use this plan?

- *You have a weakness that is creating a problem, but you can make up for it with one of your strengths.* Overall, you have many things going for you. You have a healthy reserve of skills. You are resourceful, so you can easily access areas where you are strong to serve as stand-ins for a lack of skill.

- *You have limited time and energy to invest in self-development—not every weakness makes the cut.* Creating your improvement plan requires careful consideration and prioritization. Inevitably, you will have some weaknesses that are not important enough to invest in developing, but you need to do something so that the weakness does not overshadow your strengths. You want people to focus on what you're doing well, not the distractions the weakness may be causing.

- *You have worked on developing this skill but progress is slow, you have lost motivation, or you need to buy some time.* Perhaps this skill has made it into your Development plan in years past and either it's harder to develop than you thought or you're just not seeing the progress you need to see. The Substitution plan can act as an interim plan—or a proxy—to rely on while you shore up your plan to develop.

How do I use this plan?

The goal is to get the work done and reduce the noise—to neutralize the impact of the weakness rather than working directly on the weakness. Look at other things you may be good at that you could rely on to fill the need.

This plan requires you to identify viable substitutes—skills are not all interchangeable. There is a science behind how different skills are related and which ones can substitute for others. The trick is knowing which skills serve as suitable substitutes for your area of weakness. If you struggle with Creativity, using your strength in Problem solving will be more helpful than your ability to stay composed. You can think about substitute competencies in these categories:

- *Related substitutes* cover the same territory but in a slightly different way. For example, Approachability as a substitute for Interpersonal savvy.

- *Counter substitutes* cover the missing skill with something that lessens its impact. Substituting Humor for Presentation skills is a good example of a counter substitute.

- *Diverting substitutes* divert attention away from the first goal and substitute another equally important goal in its place. The diverting substitute draws attention away from the negative impact of the weakness—it could be seen as a redeeming quality. For example, substituting Organizing (marshalling and orchestrating resources to get things done) for Interpersonal savvy. While you might not have done it in a "nice" way, you get good things done.

In many cases, using your intuition and trial and error will help you find an appropriate alternative for your weak area. However, there is a science to it, and if you want to save yourself some guesswork, use *FYI® For Your Improvement* 5th Edition to find several substitute competencies under the Unskilled definition section for each competency.

Let's say that you're simply not an effective presenter—you know it, the people nodding off in the back row know it, and the people who keep checking their mobile devices know it. You could go to a presentation skills seminar, or you could read a book on making effective presentations, but you've tried both of those before and you just haven't gleaned enough from those experiences to make a real difference.

In short, you've tried to work directly on the weakness, it hasn't worked, and you're not motivated to go there again. You've ruled out a Development plan. It's also not something you can pass off to someone else because it's in your area of expertise and responsibility, so you can forget about the Workaround plan too. But all hope is not lost. You are good at organizing information and managing process. Plus, your sense of humor frequently lightens the mood around the office.

You could substitute these strengths to attack a weakness in Presentation skills by writing out your key points, distributing them ahead of the meeting, structuring the presentation to accommodate more dialogue, and strategically inserting humor. Again, the outcome is to reduce the impact of being a marginal presenter by substituting things you are already good at to get the same thing done. This approach is relatively easy to do if you have the skills necessary to counter your need.

Is this avoiding the problem? Well, it depends on how you define the problem. If you define the problem as failing to achieve a goal, a desired outcome, then substituting another skill is an efficient and effective way to tackle the problem You're going to use your strengths to achieve the same end.

So, what's the more pressing goal? Fixing all of your weaknesses or finding a better way to do a great job? Being more effective at work doesn't require that you eliminate every weakness—only that you neutralize the ones that are having a negative impact.

Example

Even though Tamara will be celebrating 15 years with her company this spring, she has a tough time navigating the organization and getting approval from the right people at the right time. It could be due, in part, to her disdain for anything procedural and her disregard for governance. Her preference is to get the work done as efficiently as possible. But, of course, in any organization, especially larger organizations, getting the work done can involve knocking on a lot of doors and involving many people from different departments.

Recently, Tamara was promoted to VP of Communications, and she is taking a close look at success factors for her new role. Organizational agility is in the top 10. In the past, she's used a Workaround plan and relied on others (usually her boss) to be her guide to navigating the organization. Now that she's the boss, it's time for her to step up her game in that area. Tamara knows that her biggest barrier to developing this skill has been her lack of patience with maneuvering through the organization. Frankly, she'd rather find a suitable substitute that can cover for her lack of Organizational agility.

She pulls her tattered, dog-eared *FYI® For Your Improvement* 5th Edition book off her shelf and finds what substitutes might work. Understanding others and Comfort around higher management strike her as good candidates to consider. Tamara has always had a knack for reading the needs of different groups. If she can use her skill in Understanding others to anticipate concerns and interests of different stakeholder groups, it will help her move her priorities through the organizational maze. Tamara is also skilled in Comfort around higher management. Particularly helpful is her ability to understand how senior managers think and operate. These two skills will keep her thinking in a proactive manner so she can advance her strategic objectives and get the results she's hoping to achieve.

| 33

Paths to improvement plan

Paths to improvement plan

Name: *Tamara*   Date to be completed by: *December*

1 What is the GAP?

Organizational agility
I just can't get motivated to get my work reviewed and approved by the appropriate people. I have tripped up in the past because I haven't worked across departmental boundaries very well. I find that the complexity just frustrates me.

2 What is the GOAL?

I really need to be able to navigate the organization in my new role as VP of Communications. Organizational agility is critically important, but I don't think I would be successful developing it.

3 How will I get there? What PATH will I take?

Deeper exploration
- ☐ Insight plan
- ☐ Exposure plan

Direct skill building
- ☐ Development plan
- ☐ Enhancement plan
- ☐ Good to extraordinary plan
- ☐ Rerailment plan

Alternative paths
- ☑ Substitution plan
- ☐ Workaround plan
- ☐ Compensation plan

Demonstrating skill
- ☐ Marketing plan
- ☐ Skill transfer plan
- ☐ Confidence building plan

Accepting the consequences
- ☐ Redeployment plan
- ☐ Capitulation plan

4 What is my PLAN? What are my action steps?

I will rely on my strengths in Understanding others and Comfort around higher management. As I move projects along, I will proactively analyze stakeholder groups to understand their interests and concerns and anticipate how they might perceive or react to these initiatives.

5 What is the TIME LINE?

I have a 90-day agenda for onboarding in my new role. I would like to have an appropriate substitute in place and functioning for my lack of Organizational agility within the next 90 days.

8 Workaround plan

Use someone or something else to
get the same thing done.

"Most of us need the crutch at times;
but of course it is idiotic to use the crutch
when our own legs can do the journey on their own.**"**

Clive Staples Lewis – Irish-born British author

What is the Workaround plan?

The Workaround plan will help you neutralize your weakness by relying on other resources to get the same thing done. In this plan, you admit your weakness and work aggressively to find another way to accomplish what is required. You could use other people, change tasks, change your job, or use your self-awareness to work around your lack of skill. It's possible but not guaranteed that you would learn something while using a workaround strategy. The focus here is on accomplishing what needs to be done without directly addressing the weakness.

When do I use this plan?

Many successful people have, at times, had to work around a weakness. They had to find other resources and ways to get done what needed to be done. That's not to say we're advocating that you ignore your development needs or take the easy route. On the contrary, we're suggesting that there are other ways of meeting the requirements. Here are two situations where a Workaround plan is appropriate:

- *You don't have time to fix a weakness.* Perhaps your situation does not afford you the time to work on the weakness. You're on a tight deadline and urgent circumstances demand adequate or better performance right now. Or you lack a skill that is very difficult to develop and it will take time. Either way, it is clear that you will not be the one to do the work yourself.

- *You have tried to develop a weakness and you have not been successful.* When there is an aspect of your job that you are not particularly good at— which you know you will never be great at—you could benefit from finding a way around it. Maybe you lack the motivation, willingness, or opportunity to improve. Or maybe you have put a lot of effort into building the skill but it doesn't seem to be in the cards for you. Regardless, you would see better results if you work around your weakness.

How do I use this plan?

So, where do you start? Where successful people start: with self-knowledge. Admit what others probably already know: here's something you're not especially good at, but it's critical to your success. What are your realistic options for meeting the need (achieving the desired outcome)? There are four primary types of Workarounds: People, Task, Change, and Self.

- *People workarounds.* Find an internal or external person to stand in for you when the weakness is in play. This could be a peer, a friend, someone from your staff, or a consultant. For example, if you are a marginal presenter, get someone who is a good presenter to present your material. Hire people for your team who are good in the areas you are not. Delegate the tasks that bring the weakness into play.

- *Task workarounds.* Trade tasks or share tasks with a peer. For example, you help a peer with strategic planning, and they help you with presentations to senior management. Structure the weakness out. Redesign your job (with your boss) so that you are not responsible for the task(s) that brings your weakness into play. Change your job so that you no longer have to give lots of speeches to strangers. Assign that task to another unit.

- *Change workarounds.* If you decide that you don't want to work on your needs, do an honest assessment of your strengths and find an organization, a job, another unit, or another career that fits those strengths (see also the Redeployment plan, page 61). If you are in sales promotion and are not a comfortable presenter or cold caller, then find a sales job where leads are provided or customers come to you, or consider marketing analysis where those two requirements are greatly decreased.

- *Self workarounds.* Acknowledge your weaknesses and be honest with yourself and others. Research shows that admitting weaknesses (within limits) actually increases people's evaluations of you and respect for you. So if you start by saying, "As most of you know, public speaking is not one of my strengths," people will not be as critical. Redefine yourself and make a conscious decision to live with a weakness. If you decide not to address the need directly, concentrate harder on the things you do well.

Regardless of the approach, workarounds are all intended to accomplish one goal: reduce the noise while enabling you to determine the best way to get the job done. Become great at what you're good at, and find ways to work around what you're not.

Example

Allan is a product developer at a very lean company who has been moved into the role of product manager, almost without knowing it. He's strong in the development of strategy. He's an out-of-the-box creative thinker. He's good at managing innovation. He has a great sense of humor, plenty of intellectual horsepower, and is an agile learner. Among other strengths are Managerial courage, Standing alone, and Written communications.

He is aware, from personal reflection, that there is room for improvement in the areas of Listening, Delegation, Career ambition, being Action oriented, and Business acumen. And feedback has also confirmed that he's weaker in those areas.

Yesterday, Allan submitted a project plan which he had labored over for several days, focusing on the smallest details because he knew how important it was to get it right. Today when he got to work, he learned that his boss wants him to convert the plan into a pro forma statement.

Since Allan is not quite sure what converting the plan into a pro forma statement involves, he begins by searching MBA web sites for help. The problem is, his boss wants a quick turnaround on this request.

Allan knows, as others endorse, that he can implement business strategy with the best of them. It's just that he lacks Business acumen, whether by personality or inclination. Education and experience haven't molded him into a business savvy person either. Upon reflection, Allan thinks that his best chance at delivering the result his boss wants to see is by relying on other people. He's choosing to work with his friend in finance and another peer in strategic planning to shape this plan into a pro forma statement.

Paths to improvement plan

Paths to improvement plan

Name: _Allan_   Date to be completed by: _October_

1 What is the **GAP?**

Business acumen
My Business acumen is not strong enough to create detailed strategic plans and financial projections.

2 What is the **GOAL?**

My boss is asking me to deliver a pro forma statement by the end of the month. I don't have time to learn how to do this. I think I need to call in a favor.

3 How will I get there? What **PATH** will I take?

Deeper exploration
- ☐ Insight plan
- ☐ Exposure plan

Direct skill building
- ☐ Development plan
- ☐ Enhancement plan
- ☐ Good to extraordinary plan
- ☐ Rerailment plan

Alternative paths
- ☐ Substitution plan
- ☒ Workaround plan
- ☐ Compensation plan

Demonstrating skill
- ☐ Marketing plan
- ☐ Skill transfer plan
- ☐ Confidence building plan

Accepting the consequences
- ☐ Redeployment plan
- ☐ Capitulation plan

4 What is my **PLAN?** What are my action steps?

I've decided on a People workaround. I've scheduled time with Betsy in Finance and Bill in Strategic Planning. They've agreed to work on the pro forma over the next couple of weeks, as long as I can provide them with the details of the project.

5 What is the **TIME LINE?**

Beginning this week and continuing over the next few months.

9 Compensation plan

Decrease the noise of an overuse.

" *Everything in moderation...including moderation.* **"**

Julia Child – American chef and author

What is the Compensation plan?

The Compensation plan will help you temper problems created by an overused strength by employing other compensating skills. The compensating skills do not accomplish the same thing as the overused strength; rather, they are auxiliary skills which cushion the blow dealt by a strength gone into overdrive. The goal is not to stop using or to dial back the overused strength; instead, it is to increase your use of other skills to intervene and deflect any negative consequences of overuse.

When do I use this plan?

Not every opportunity to improve surfaces from a weakness. In some instances, your performance can deteriorate if a strength goes into overdrive. You may be using a strength too much or too broadly. You may be using the strength in situations that do not call for it. Regardless, when strengths are overused, it can create problems for you. The Compensation plan is designed to help you identify and employ compensator skills that will moderate the overused skill. The following situations present good opportunities to apply this plan:

- *You have a strength that you are overusing that is causing noise.* It's possible to have too much of a good thing when it creates an imbalance. Humor in overdrive becomes inappropriate and potentially distracting. A strength in Customer focus becomes a problem if it means someone is willing to abandon all important policies and practices in favor of bending over backwards for the customer. A strength in Career ambition becomes a problem when it overshadows a person's attention to his current job.

- *You are having trouble adjusting how much you apply your strength.* It's not easy to be less results oriented, less courageous, less smart. You have been rewarded for these leadership qualities, and they are not something you can just turn on or off. Doing less of what you're best at is hard to accept as a strategy for improvement.

- *You are relying on your strength in inappropriate situations.* You may have some very admirable qualities—like Compassion or Patience. While you don't want to lessen your skill in these areas, these qualities can be counterproductive in situations like meeting critical deadlines, providing tough feedback, or being firm with expectations.

- *You are faced with new expectations but continue to use strengths that made you successful in the past.* A strength can kick into overdrive at any time, but especially when a new situation or context calls for a strength you don't have. This often occurs when individuals are promoted from individual contributor to manager, or from manager of a team to head of a department. These transitions require a shift in which skills you employ.

When strengths go into overdrive, it makes sense to look for other alternatives—or compensators—other things you are good at that can be better engaged to temper your overused strength or reduce the noise it generates.

How do I use this plan?

First, you will probably need to ask for more feedback (either with a formal 360° multi-rater feedback process or in the course of informal conversations). It is very difficult to recognize when your strengths go into overdrive because you are accustomed to viewing them in such a positive light. Be ready to recognize and overcome your resistance to hearing that you are overusing a strength—it's not easy to receive constructive feedback when your intentions are good and your skill level is high.

Once you've identified overused strengths that might be creating some noise, you can refer to *FYI® For Your Improvement* 5th Edition to see the list of compensators that can mitigate overuse. Typically, it takes from one to three compensators to balance an overused strength, that is, to reduce the noise it generates. Engage these compensator strengths by focusing on how well and how frequently you employ them. Once you have identified effective compensator skills, create a specific plan for the overused strength that is the source of the problem.

If you're not sure what your specific overused strength is, or you want to inoculate yourself against the likelihood of a problem caused by overuse, you could focus on the "saving graces."

These are the eight "saving grace" skills that are especially effective at helping other people overlook various faults and covering up many different problems:

- Approachability – being warm.
- Boss relationships – working well with your boss.
- Compassion – feeling other people's pain and trying to help.
- Humor – making "heavy" situations lighter.
- Integrity and trust – being direct, honest, and forthright.
- Interpersonal savvy – relating well to others.
- Listening – being open to input.
- Understanding others – knowing why groups of people do similar things.

Of the eight saving graces, Listening is by far the most powerful compensator. However, all eight saving grace skills serve as balancers so your strengths don't shift into overuse and become weaknesses. Saving graces are the most frequently mentioned positives after the "buts" in organizations. As in, "So-and-so can be awfully short with people and gruff, but underneath he's got a heart of gold when you really get to know him."

In some organizations, saving graces lead to long and maybe lifelong tenure and staying power. Saving graces can compensate for mistakes that would get others without them into career trouble. Those with saving graces tend to form multiple and long-lasting relationships throughout the organization and with external customers because they are a trusted and approachable person.

Whether you choose specific compensators for your identified overused skill, or whether you focus on saving graces, you will want to turn up the volume on the compensator skill in order to lessen the noise of overuse.

Example

Seth, a manager, is typically thought of as someone who does not hesitate to take action. He is known for his tendency to fearlessly jump in and work hard. Folks can count on him to take initiative and seize opportunities. His energetic approach is admirable and inspiring.

But on Seth's latest 360° feedback report, several raters, including his boss (who is the group executive VP), agreed that he is overusing Action oriented. Comments on the report allude to instances when he has "jumped to a solution before adequate analysis," and someone else noted that "In his zeal to get things done quickly, he neglects to address the complexity and often finds himself having to retreat and redo work."

Seth's failure to pause before he takes action is giving people the impression that he is not strategic. This is problematic for him in his current role and for his career aspirations. The coach assigned to deliver feedback to Seth is tempted to be direct and suggest, "Well look, your tendency to jump in without analyzing is not seen as a very strategic approach. Stop being so action oriented." It doesn't work that way.

So, the coach thinks, "Hmm, I wonder what else he might be average or good at that he could further engage to compensate for the overuse in action orientation?" Seth and his coach look into compensator skills that would help temper his overuse of Action oriented.

Seth notes that Priority setting, Problem solving, and Process management are among his average skills—raters thought he was skilled in these areas. He also discovers (by turning to the Action oriented chapter in his *FYI® For Your Improvement* 5th Edition book) that these are three of the compensators recommended to temper overuse in Action oriented. Seth figures that he could find ways to better engage these skills.

Seth chooses to compensate for overusing Action oriented by stepping up his use of Priority setting and Problem solving. By building some discipline around sorting through the critical tasks and the trivial tasks, he will use his time more strategically. By anticipating roadblocks and doing some honest analysis prior to diving in, he will ensure that his effort will not be lost. Seth is relieved that his coach is not asking him to sit on his hands or hold back. It would be against his nature to not take action. Instead, Seth will use a compensation approach to neutralize the effect of overusing a strength. He will do this by better engaging other skills he is good at that will complement and balance out his overused strength.

43

Paths to improvement plan

Paths to improvement plan

Name: _Seth_   Date to be completed by: _April_

1 What is the **GAP?**	_Action oriented_ _I just got feedback that my action orientation is becoming a barrier because I am not acting strategically, and I am creating rework for myself and others._
2 What is the **GOAL?**	_I'm really proud of my ability to take initiative. I don't want it to turn into a liability. I need to figure out a new approach that will allow me to use my strength and let it bolster rather than impede my efforts at work._

3 How will I get there? What **PATH** will I take?

Deeper exploration
- ☐ Insight plan
- ☐ Exposure plan

Direct skill building
- ☐ Development plan
- ☐ Enhancement plan
- ☐ Good to extraordinary plan
- ☐ Rerailment plan

Alternative paths
- ☐ Substitution plan
- ☐ Workaround plan
- ☒ Compensation plan

Demonstrating skill
- ☐ Marketing plan
- ☐ Skill transfer plan
- ☐ Confidence building plan

Accepting the consequences
- ☐ Redeployment plan
- ☐ Capitulation plan

4 What is my **PLAN?** What are my action steps?	_I know I'm good at Priority setting, Problem solving, and Process management. I guess I just haven't used them as much as I've relied on being Action oriented. I think I can use these—particularly Priority setting and Problem solving—to channel my actions and direct my activities more strategically. The goal is to complement my action orientation so it doesn't go into overdrive._
5 What is the **TIME LINE?**	_My team has a couple of key milestones in April. I'd like to temper my use of action orientation and see the amount of rework and wasted effort go down._

Demonstrating skill

10	Marketing plan
11	Skill Transfer plan
12	Confidence building plan

In some cases, you are skilled in an area but your ability is not apparent to you or others. Perhaps you have used the skill outside of work, at a former company, or in a previous role. You need to demonstrate your ability in order to convince yourself or others that you are skilled. It could be a matter of building self-confidence, marketing yourself, or transferring your skill from one context to another.

10 Marketing plan

Let others know you are skilled in an area.

" As we let our own light shine, we unconsciously give other people permission to do the same."

Nelson Mandela – Anti-apartheid activist and former president of South Africa

What is the Marketing plan?

The Marketing plan will help you to persuade others that you really do have a particular skill. It addresses the perception gap that exists when you truly are skilled in an area but others do not perceive that you are. Once the perception gap is corrected, you can be sure that critical decisions related to work assignments, promotions, and raises will be based on your actual ability.

When do I use this plan?

- *There is a perception gap—others do not know you are skilled in an area.* There are times when you will find yourself rejecting the perceptions of others about your skill level in a critical area. You know you are skilled in a mission-critical area, but not everyone is aware that you have the skill. If what you're doing is mission-critical and you're doing it well, people ought to know about it.

- *There are inconsistencies in how different groups view your skill level— some think you're good at it, others do not see it.* You are skilled in a mission-critical area and certain individuals or groups rate you lower than other groups. It could be that some people see the skill in action while other people do not. For example, your boss may not think you are great at Delegation, but you and your direct reports know that it's a strength. Or your direct reports think you are weak in Standing alone and Managerial courage, but higher management knows that you excel in this area.

- *You were rated high in a skill at a previous company, but in your current organization you don't have a chance to use it.* The strengths you employ depend on the context. The gap in perception could be explained by the environment or the situation. For example, in your old job, you may have been in charge of strategy. In your new job, you may be focused on execution excellence. Each situation emphasizes different skills in order to be successful. Your new colleagues might not see your strategic agility because you are focused on a different set of goals.

How do I use this plan?

Before you get started, be sure of two things: One, the skill in question is actually important. People are going to care whether you are good or not because it's a critical part of your job and it supports achieving the company's goals. Two, be sure that you are actually good at the skill. If there is no substance behind your claim, your colleagues will pick up on that fact very quickly. Advertising something you don't have will be more damaging to your reputation than the initial problem you were trying to solve. Recovering from this misrepresentation of your skill, whether it's due to low self-awareness or lack of humility, will require patient and deliberate rebuilding of trust. Once you are sure that those two things are in place—the skill is mission critical and it's something you really are good at—you are ready to embark on your Marketing plan.

Marketing is a matter of shaping perception. The primary tools for doing this are communication and demonstration. Communication could involve simple sound-bite advertisements for your skill: "I really enjoy solving problems—I think it's one of my strengths." Or you could be less direct: "That's a tough problem, but I've got a framework in mind that will help me analyze it and come up with some possible solutions." Either way, you are planting the seeds that will build your brand as a problem solver.

Demonstration of the skill is even more important. You are building credibility. If you want people to believe that you are actually good at the skill, they need to see it. While you haven't been known for this skill up to this point, this is your opportunity to prove yourself.

- *Find an opportunity to use your skill and use it often.* Whether it is a core part of your job or not, find a project or other activity that will give you the opportunity to showcase your skill in the area.

- *Let others see you in action.* If your boss questions your ability to focus on the customer, invite them along on a sales call. Point out why you chose to approach the conversation the way you did and offer to provide updates on that customer relationship.

- *Get people involved with you so they see what you're doing behind the scenes.* Others cannot read your mind, and they don't know what you do after hours or behind a closed office door. Open up. Share your thought process. Walk them through the steps you take. Have a working session that highlights the contribution you make to a collaborative effort.

- *Help others make the link between your actions and the positive results you're getting.* Let's say your direct reports uniformly view you as weak on Standing alone, and it's affecting their confidence in your leadership. Let them know through informational briefings what you're doing in this area. Talk about the courageous stands you have taken on behalf of your department. Share with them how you were a champion for an idea which led to a positive result for the team.

Sharing your skill with others not only benefits your personal brand, it can help others learn and improve.

Example

In his first 360° report, Manuel received a relatively low score on Creativity—compared to other skills, it was ranked very low. He is visibly disappointed with his score in that area. It is a skill he is proud of and one that he thinks is critical to the success of his business unit. The one encouraging piece of news is that his peers consider him to be "talented" in Creativity.

As he explores this result with a colleague, he shares that he was considered to be extremely creative in his last job, which was in marketing. Now that he's in communications, he realizes that most of his focus is on planning, wrangling stakeholders, and putting out fires. It occurs to him that while his peers see him work through the creative process during brainstorming sessions and reviewing his writing, he doesn't showcase that skill to his boss, direct reports, or customers.

The reflective conversation crystallizes how strongly Manuel feels about his creative ability. Being creative is a tremendous source of job satisfaction and closely tied to his identity. He firmly believes his creativity can positively shape his role and contribution to the company. He is committed to make it part of his personal brand.

Paths to improvement plan

Paths to improvement plan

Name: *Manuel*   Date to be completed by: *April*

1 What is the GAP?

Creativity
All others (boss, direct reports, customers) do not see Creativity as one of my top skills, while my peers and I do.

2 What is the GOAL?

I think creativity is one key ingredient to handling or avoiding crises. I have seen how my creative nature has had an impact in marketing, and I'd like creativity to contribute in a similar way to my work in communications.

3 How will I get there? What PATH will I take?

Deeper exploration
☐ Insight plan
☐ Exposure plan

Direct skill building
☐ Development plan
☐ Enhancement plan
☐ Good to extraordinary plan
☐ Rerailment plan

Alternative paths
☐ Substitution plan
☐ Workaround plan
☐ Compensation plan

Demonstrating skill
☒ Marketing plan
☐ Skill transfer plan
☐ Confidence building plan

Accepting the consequences
☐ Redeployment plan
☐ Capitulation plan

4 What is my PLAN? What are my action steps?

Communications has been asked to do some internal branding work to increase employee engagement. Specifically, the executive leadership team would like to move the needle on the engagement driver related to employees having personal influence in the business. I have a lot of creative ideas that could shape this initiative. I will first work to convince my boss that I have had successful creative ideas in the past. Then, I will engage my team in a series of brainstorming meetings. Once we have our creative ideas hammered out, I will be clear in taking personal ownership for the success (or failure) of my creative contribution. I think this will build my credibility and brand as a creative contributor.

5 What is the TIME LINE?

I think I can tackle this in 2–3 months.

11 Skill transfer plan

Take what is working in one context
and transfer it to another.

*❝I'm learning real skills that I can apply throughout
the rest of my life...procrastinating and rationalizing.❞*

Bill Watterson — American cartoonist and author of *Calvin and Hobbes*

What is the Skill transfer plan?

The Skill transfer plan will help you take a skill you use in one setting and apply it in a different setting. You may find that you partition your life into different segments—there's family, work, volunteering, hobbies, and other interests. It's not uncommon for a person to use certain skills in one area of life and not in others. This plan helps you identify where you already employ skills that are needed in another area. That way, you can transfer them across boundaries and bring more of yourself to work.

When do I use this plan?

* *You do not show evidence of a skill in one context, but you rely on it in a different setting.* Perhaps you think the skill is irrelevant or even discouraged at work, or maybe you lack the confidence to apply it in the work setting. If the absence of the skill is getting noticed, and the presence of the skill would benefit you and the work you do, it's time to break down the barrier and let it shine at work. For example, one individual in a highly technical role finds herself pursuing a variety of artistic interests outside of work. For all the time she spends painting, firing pottery, and installing her work at local art galleries, she never considers the value her creativity would bring to her day job. In fact, the technical problems she encounters would benefit from her unique ideas and her ability to brainstorm and make connections between seemingly unrelated notions. Transferring her creativity from her off-work activities and applying it at work will reap tremendous benefits.

* *You are a different person when you're in your comfort zone or when the stakes are lower.* For example, you may receive feedback that you do not take charge enough at work—that you lack assertiveness. Yet at the Thursday night softball league, you're clearly the team captain—always conferring with the pitcher on strategy, deciding on the batting order, and standing up to the umpire when there are questionable calls. So, what's

happening here? It's a matter of comfort. At the softball game, where the stakes are known and low, you are in your comfort zone and naturally take command. At work, you may be less inclined to take a public or assertive stand unless you are absolutely certain about the issue at hand. Or, for any number of reasons, the work environment may not bring out the best in you.

How do I use this plan?

When you discover a weakness or a need at work, pause to think before you pursue a plan to address that skill. Think about yourself more holistically. Think about things you have achieved and how you have accomplished them. Take a look at your resume. Do a mental review of high and low points throughout your life. It may be helpful to have a friend, mentor, or coach prompt your thinking by asking you questions. Think about the skill and what it would look like if you were good at it outside of work. Then, ask yourself and others whether you have shown evidence of that skill in any non-work arenas.

Getting some general feedback from people who know you outside of work can be enlightening as well. Ask family members and long-time friends about what you do well. Often a spouse or partner can help you identify the skills that you use outside of work. You could even have a close friend complete a leadership or personality assessment on you to see what their feedback highlights. Compare this feedback with what you're hearing at work and reflect on any discrepancies.

Participate in a leadership course or coaching program that addresses the whole person. This may involve taking some personality assessments, participating in life interviews, or completing self-reflection exercises. While these experiences may push you out of your comfort zone, keep your goal in mind—to discover strengths that you have outside of work that could help you excel if you begin to bring them to work.

Example

Kate has heard through the grapevine that people find her to be a bit cold and unfeeling at work. It's reached a point where people dread status meetings with her because she is results-driven without considering the human side of running her business unit. While it's no excuse, she has tremendous responsibility in her new role, which was previously two jobs before the company restructured. Often, she is double- or triple-booked, and lately she feels that she needs to schedule time to sneeze.

Kate confides in her coach. She tells her coach about the rumors she's hearing but also that caring about other people and being compassionate are core values for her personally. Outside of work she is committed to many social justice issues—from housing, to education, to microlending. She has been known to spend her vacation time working on Habitat for Humanity houses.

Last year she was a delegate to the international microfinance summit and met the founder of the Grameen Bank—a microfinance organization focused on community development. By far, the most rewarding thing in her volunteer efforts is the opportunity to meet and get to know the women and families that are improving their lives with support from these organizations.

So, to be seen as uncaring or lacking compassion at work is something Kate wants to remedy—it doesn't match who she wants to be, and it is an impediment to working with and through others. Kate creates a Skill transfer plan.

Paths to improvement plan

Paths to improvement plan

Name: _Kate_   Date to be completed by: _November_

1 What is the GAP?

Caring about direct reports; Compassion
I am seen as unfeeling and uncaring by people in my organization.
I am driving results and deadlines without spending enough time and
effort on the people side—making people feel appreciated, cared for,
engaged.

2 What is the GOAL?

Obviously, I have been focused on other things at work and
downplayed the importance of caring and compassion, but it appears
that an absence of those things is detrimental to getting work done
with and through others.

3 How will I get there? What PATH will I take?

Deeper exploration
- ☐ Insight plan
- ☐ Exposure plan

Direct skill building
- ☐ Development plan
- ☐ Enhancement plan
- ☐ Good to extraordinary plan
- ☐ Rerailment plan

Alternative paths
- ☐ Substitution plan
- ☐ Workaround plan
- ☐ Compensation plan

Demonstrating skill
- ☐ Marketing plan
- ☒ Skill transfer plan
- ☐ Confidence building plan

Accepting the consequences
- ☐ Redeployment plan
- ☐ Capitulation plan

4 What is my PLAN? What are my action steps?

One of the things I do really well in my volunteer work is listening
without judging. I think that will help people feel that I am
empathetic. I'm also very curious about other people outside of
work—I think I can transfer that by getting curious about how
people think and asking them "What if?" "What would you change?"
"How did you come to that?" I think these behaviors will help people
feel that I value and care about them.

5 What is the TIME LINE?

Within a few months, I would like to see some shift in others'
perceptions. I think it needs to be somewhat gradual rather than a
flip of a switch. I need to get the hang of what it looks like to be
caring at work, and others need to know that it's authentic.

12 Confidence building plan

Build confidence in your ability.

What is the Confidence building plan?

The Confidence building plan will help you build your self-confidence in an area where you are strong but lack confidence. Other people see that the area is a strength for you, but you feel less sure of your ability. The Confidence building plan helps you believe in your ability when you don't seem to know how good you are—or could be—at something. Hidden strengths are the skills you have but underestimate. When you have a hidden strength or people see potential that you don't see, you risk expending needless energy fixing something that isn't broken or underusing a critical skill. Others already know you're good at it—now it's just a matter of helping you to know.

When do I use this plan?

- *You have a strength but your lack of confidence is holding you back.* This could be a case of excessive humility or exceedingly high expectations. Or it's possible that you are surrounded by extremely talented people, and you feel like you don't measure up. Deeper, it's sometimes the result of having parents with unreasonable standards and/or brothers and sisters who have achieved more than you have. Regardless of the reason, a lack of self-confidence is more common when you are in the early- to middle stages of your career. As you go higher up the leadership chain, problems of low self-confidence are less likely; after all, it takes a good amount of self-confidence to continue to climb the corporate ladder.

- *You have a hidden strength—a skill that others see that you do not see.* You are not aware of how brightly you shine, or could shine. Maybe you don't know how good you really are in comparison to others. You need to believe in your ability to fully utilize your skill. You probably need to seek additional feedback. Have other people point out when they see you demonstrate the skill. Get into situations that require the skill so you can get quality, timely feedback from people you respect. Build awareness of your ability.

How do I use this plan?

Figure out why you lack confidence in a particular skill. Did you have a bad experience or an early failure? Do you have unrealistically high standards for yourself? Are you clueless about how you compare to others in this area? Are you reluctant to disclose your ability because people might expect more from you? Understanding the underlying cause of your lack of self-confidence can help you overcome your hesitance to use the skill.

Seek additional feedback from others—especially those whose perspectives you really trust. Ideally, find the peer, boss, or mentor who is not always overly positive and not likely to say something just to flatter you. Understand the specifics of the behaviors they see that indicate a high level of skill in a particular area. Take care not to be dismissive of the feedback. Rather, try to view it somewhat objectively. Review the tapes in your memory so you can see what you're doing that is working.

Identify potential situations that would allow you to test-drive or showcase your skill. Ideally, these would be assignments or projects where you receive adequate but gradually diminishing support from trusted colleagues or mentors. As you gain your footing, you will need less reassurance and eventually be ready to fly without a net.

Example

Rachel is in the research group at a major think tank based in Singapore. She was recruited out of graduate school a few years ago because the group found her to be incredibly adept at research design and decision quality. Most people in her lab at graduate school came to her for advice and counsel because she offered wise analysis and good judgment. She didn't think much of it, just that she was doing her part as a research partner in the lab. Her current workgroup views her the same way that her graduate-student colleagues did. Even though she is the junior member of the team, they really value her perspective—she often catches things they wouldn't think of.

Rachel's team is almost ready to launch a major study, but she sees a few flaws in the way they are gathering the data. In fact, she's pretty sure that the approach they are taking will lead to significant problems later on in the analysis phase. Unfortunately, she keeps this to herself because she doesn't feel confident enough in her opinion to speak up. She figures that she is surrounded by experienced researchers who know a lot more than she does about conducting this type of study.

After six months of data gathering go by, Rachel casually shares this insight with her boss, privately. Her boss rightly asks her why she took so long to point out the flawed design, and he gives Rachel specific examples where she has demonstrated a strength in this area. After some dialogue, Rachel realizes that she didn't think she offered any unique perspective or gifted ability in the area of wisdom, analysis, or judgment. And, in the past, she has only offered her advice when it was solicited directly. It is news to her that people consider her to be very talented in quality decision making. She never considered herself to be especially distinguished in that area.

Paths to improvement plan

Paths to improvement plan

Name: *Rachel*   Date to be completed by: *June*

1 What is the **GAP?**	*Decision quality* *I need to learn to view my ability to analyze, deliberate, and make sound judgments as a strength, compared to others.*
2 What is the **GOAL?**	*Unless I begin to view myself as a gifted decision maker, I will not be able to fully contribute my talents to the team.*

3 How will I get there? What **PATH** will I take?

Deeper exploration
- ☐ Insight plan
- ☐ Exposure plan

Direct skill building
- ☐ Development plan
- ☐ Enhancement plan
- ☐ Good to extraordinary plan
- ☐ Rerailment plan

Alternative paths
- ☐ Substitution plan
- ☐ Workaround plan
- ☐ Compensation plan

Demonstrating skill
- ☐ Marketing plan
- ☐ Skill transfer plan
- ☒ Confidence building plan

Accepting the consequences
- ☐ Redeployment plan
- ☐ Capitulation plan

4 What is my **PLAN?** What are my action steps?	*I have been given the opportunity to be the research lead on our next major study. My boss assures me that he will be right by my side encouraging me to share my judgments and suggestions in a more forthright and confident manner. We have established a few milestone checkpoints that will help us measure whether my judgment and my leadership of the project are on the right track. This will build my confidence and mitigate risk by allowing for course corrections along the way.*
5 What is the **TIME LINE?**	*I'm giving myself 6 months to work on this during the launch phase of our next major study.*

Accepting the consequences

13 Redeployment plan

14 Capitulation plan

After exhausting other options, it may become clear that improving a mission-critical skill or changing your skill portfolio is not likely. You have reached the end of the road in your efforts to improve in your current role. You are ready to accept the reality that you are not in the right role. The choice at this point is Redeployment (find a better fit) or Capitulation (do nothing). And, as with all choices, there are implications with either path you choose.

13 Redeployment plan

Find a better match.

> *"Wherever you fly, you'll be best of the best.*
> *Wherever you go, you will top all the rest.*
> *Except when you don't. Because sometimes you won't.*
> *...And the chances are, then, that you'll be in a slump.*
> *And when you're in a slump you're not in for much fun.*
> *Un-slumping yourself is not easily done."*

Dr. Seuss – American author and artist

What is the Redeployment plan?

The Redeployment plan helps you to acknowledge that you are not in the right role and documents a series of steps to find a better match for your skills and interests. It's a plan that guides your career path. While it may not be the path that leads you significantly higher in your organization, it has the virtues of helping you find a place that's a better fit for you and one where you can add more value to the organization.

When do I use this plan?

- *Your strengths are not important or useful in your current job.* Suppose you look at your profile of strengths and weaknesses and it confirms something you've sort of known but haven't really confronted: the things you're best at aren't going to make you a star in your current role, and the skills you are weaker in are the ones that matter most. Adopting the approach of focusing solely on strengths and ignoring your weaknesses isn't going to get you anywhere in this role because your strengths, while admirable, are clearly not mission critical. So, how about finding a role, a department, a culture, or a job that better suits your profile?

- *You think it's unlikely that you will change to fit the job requirements.* Perhaps you have tried to use a substitution or workaround approach to deal with the mismatch between your skill set and your role—but these don't seem like permanent solutions. Perhaps you have tried (unsuccessfully) to develop some of the mission-critical skills where you are weak. Or perhaps you are not motivated or not interested in changing to meet the needs of

| 61

the role. At some point, you recognize that if you cannot, will not, or do not want to change, then something else has to change. Namely, your job.

• *The organization you work for has gone through a significant change and you no longer fit in or want to fit in.* Something has happened. Perhaps it's a merger or acquisition. Maybe the organization is downsizing. There could be new leadership, a new CEO, a different board. It's possible that a change in direction or strategic vision is taking place. Maybe your sponsor has left. Whatever the cause, you no longer fit in comfortably. The things that made you successful in the past will no longer play as well. Your experience is no longer valued.

How do I use this plan?

First, get a clear understanding of your strengths and interests. If you haven't already done so, get feedback from people you work with—either informally or through a formal 360° multi-rater assessment. If possible, consider taking an interest inventory or aptitude test. These can help you discern your skill and interest profile. Next, find the jobs or careers where your strengths would be mission critical. Job descriptions usually list the most important skills for the role. Your HR department can also review the skill requirements for different roles, levels, and departments.

Change jobs. Ideally, you will find a job where your strengths and the needs of the organization intersect. Let's say you're a brilliant engineer who has been a solid team member on sizeable projects; then you get promoted to a team leadership job and find that you're failing because you lack the skills to manage conflict and develop direct reports. You know that these are not only areas that are relatively hard to develop, but from reflecting on experience, you realize that you don't have an appetite for leadership. It probably makes sense to find another job as an individual contributor or team member where you can add value to the organization.

Change careers. There's always the chance, of course, that if you don't want to address a need in your job, you may not be able to simply change jobs. What if, for example, you were a terrific salesperson at your company based on your ability to analyze client data, propose solutions, and build lasting customer relationships, but the majority of the job required you to generate leads through cold calling. Think about what other career might allow you to better capitalize on your strengths without engaging your weaknesses. A career that emphasizes consulting over sales would be a better fit. Or maybe your strengths in business acumen, problem solving, and managing relationships are a perfect foundation to start a new career in financial services or retail management.

Example

Mateo was a product manager at a large retail company. The products in the category he managed were performing below average to average. He struggled to meet and didn't come close to exceeding his targets. During performance reviews, he found that he was receiving below-target ratings and getting constructive feedback from his boss related to most of his goals.

The one bright spot in these performance reviews related to minor extracurricular projects Mateo was pursuing. He was a whiz with data analysis and had a passion for sharing his knowledge with others. Through a series of brown-bag sessions, he trained his entire department on using new macros that he had developed.

As part of a manager training course, Mateo received 360° feedback which didn't surprise him. He was strong in Technical learning, Developing direct reports and others, and Presentation skills. Unfortunately, he was weak in many of the skills that his boss viewed as critical to success as a product manager. These weaknesses included Business acumen, Decision quality, and Strategic agility.

After some deliberation with his feedback coach, his boss, and his spouse, Mateo recognized that his current placement just wasn't going to work out. It was a bad fit. It wasn't sustainable. And it was having a negative effect on his attitude and self-esteem. He was excelling in areas that were not important and failing in areas that were important.

While researching the company's intranet site for internal job postings, he noticed a training manager job in the Human Resource Development department that sounded as if it were fashioned just for him. It required some subject-matter expertise in the technology systems used by product managers, as well as the ability to present and explain information clearly, develop and mentor others, and create technology-enabled training courses.

Paths to improvement plan

Paths to improvement plan

Name: *Mateo*   Date to be completed by: *February*

1 What is the GAP?

Technical learning; Developing direct reports and others; Presentation skills
I have strengths that are shining in my extracurricular projects, and I would like to use them in my full-time work.

2 What is the GOAL?

Using my strengths is key to my job performance and my job satisfaction.

3 How will I get there? What PATH will I take?

Deeper exploration
☐ Insight plan
☐ Exposure plan

Direct skill building
☐ Development plan
☐ Enhancement plan
☐ Good to extraordinary plan
☐ Rerailment plan

Alternative paths
☐ Substitution plan
☐ Workaround plan
☐ Compensation plan

Demonstrating skill
☐ Marketing plan
☐ Skill transfer plan
☐ Confidence building plan

Accepting the consequences
☒ Redeployment plan
☐ Capitulation plan

4 What is my PLAN? What are my action steps?

If I need to gather some additional experience to make the transition from my current role to a new role, I will work with my boss and HR to seek out part-time assignments.

I'm going to have a career conversation with my boss. Then, I will partner with HR and explore my strengths, as well as open positions that may be good possibilities.

5 What is the TIME LINE?

In the next month or two, I would like to position myself as a strong candidate for open positions that would be a better fit for me.

14 Capitulation plan

Keep things the way they are.

I am what I am.

Gloria Gaynor – American singer

What is the Capitulation plan?

The Capitulation plan helps you understand your decision to do nothing about weaknesses or problem areas and outlines the possible consequences of inaction. Capitulation is the act of surrendering or yielding. This is less a plan and more a relinquishment. The choice here is to do nothing about any weaknesses or developmental opportunities in mission-critical areas or any other area that's causing noise.

When do I use this plan?

You agree that you have certain weaknesses that will continue to be a problem, but you are not interested in improving them. This might be related to stubbornness, lack of motivation to change, or just giving up. Choosing this approach signals that you are no longer looking to grow in your career. There are a few reasons you may choose to do nothing:

- *You don't have the resources.* Time or financial constraints could be an issue. Or perhaps your company does not invest in the training and development resources you need.

- *You don't know how to change.* Without a coach or mentor, you may feel stuck or out of ideas. Or it's possible that personal limitations make it challenging to change.

- *You are not motivated.* Your company culture may not reinforce the right rewards or social pressure to change. Or maybe you do not have a learning orientation or a focus on attaining positive outcomes.

- *You don't care about the impact on others or the organization.* Maybe you're cynical. Or relationships and the impact you have on others is not your top priority.

- *You've tried repeatedly with no results.* You have made efforts and realize that, for whatever reason, it's just not in you to improve.

How do I use this plan?

You should consider this to be your last resort. The plan is to do nothing. Work with a coach who is knowledgeable and can help you understand the possible consequences of inaction. You could be removed from a job to make room for a more ambitious individual. You could be moved to a lesser role. Or you could be fired or asked to resign. Your boss and the organization should be informed that you are choosing not to do anything to improve, as this will be seen as avoiding the issue. The choice can be managed by a very knowledgeable boss, coach, mentor, or development facilitator.

Example

Smug. That's the best word to describe Anders' demeanor. At work and off. Every day he finds something to stroke his confidence. His puffed-up nature is understandable once you realize that Anders is consistently the highest-performing salesperson on his team. He doesn't let anyone forget that his accounts are worth millions of dollars. If he ever left, he would take those connections with him.

Receiving multi-rater feedback and creating an improvement plan are not priorities in Anders' mind. No surprise that the 360° feedback report shows he is talented in Customer focus—a mission-critical skill for his role. On the flip side, he struggles with Integrity and trust as well as Composure—both important if he's going to work effectively with others and uphold the company's brand.

Anders' attitude shifts into high gear as he explains to his feedback coach that he has been successful so far and sees no need to change his behavior. "Yes, I agree that those are my strengths and weaknesses. And," pointing to a place on a chart, adding, "I don't disagree that if I don't do something to address these two areas, it's going to continue to be a problem."

Anders went on to say, "But I've gotta be honest, I've seen this same feedback over and over again, and I don't think I need to improve in the areas of Integrity and trust or Composure. I have strengths and weaknesses, just like anyone. But frankly, I can't think of anything I need to do to be more effective in my current role, and the truth is, I'm just not going to change. I like my job and I'm good at what I do. With the numbers that I produce, they can't touch me," he informs his coach.

| 67

Paths to improvement plan

Paths to improvement plan

Name: _Anders_   Date to be completed by: _Week of October 11_

1 What is the GAP?

Integrity and trust; Composure
They say that my lack of skill in these areas has impacted my reputation as well as the company's brand. Yes, I was rated low in these areas, but I still exceed my numbers every quarter.

2 What is the GOAL?

These are not so important that I can't get my job done. What I'm currently doing is getting the results I want.

3 How will I get there? What PATH will I take?

Deeper exploration
☐ Insight plan
☐ Exposure plan

Direct skill building
☐ Development plan
☐ Enhancement plan
☐ Good to extraordinary plan
☐ Rerailment plan

Alternative paths
☐ Substitution plan
☐ Workaround plan
☐ Compensation plan

Demonstrating skill
☐ Marketing plan
☐ Skill transfer plan
☐ Confidence building plan

Accepting the consequences
☐ Redeployment plan
☒ Capitulation plan

4 What is my PLAN? What are my action steps?

If my boss can't live with me the way that I am, then he will need to find a workaround that makes him comfortable. Or he can fire me.

5 What is the TIME LINE?

I will discuss the implications with my boss in our next touchbase.

A guide for coaches

As a manager, coach, mentor, or HR professional, you play an instrumental role in helping individuals grow and improve their effectiveness (De Meuse, Dai, & Lee, 2009; McCall, Lombardo, & Morrison, 1988). Research and experience suggest that there are many effective approaches to facilitating change and improvement. Depending on the individual, the situation, and the organization, the 14 paths in this book are all legitimate routes to take with individuals you are coaching. This guide is designed to provide you with some additional information and resources to help you help others.

The research chapter, "Individual improvement: A scientific examination," takes a look at the barriers and enablers of change. It reviews the individual, situational, and organizational variables that influence how easy or difficult it is for an individual to improve.

The diagnostic section, "How to select plans," takes you through a series of questions or decision points that help you determine which plan will be most helpful and effective for an individual you are coaching. Here we also provide some additional information on the features of each of the 14 paths to improvement, including the time frame, the degree of coaching support needed, and the likelihood that you will see improvement.

Finally, the ideas and ruminations found in "Coaching notes" document the collective wisdom and experience of the authors and dozens of other coaches who have experience using *Paths to improvement*. These notes provide a coaching lens through which to view each plan.

Paths to improvement: Navigating your way to success is designed to make your coaching conversations (whether they are related to career, performance, or development) as impactful as possible.

Individual improvement: A scientific examination

There is no shortage of techniques, tools, and services that promise to help us change. Self-help books and web sites abound, promising to help you shed a few pounds, drop the nicotine habit, slow down the effects of aging, or be your best self. The abundance of self-improvement resources points to two things: (1) a lot of us want to improve ourselves, and (2) it's not easy to improve and change.

The quest for self-improvement is not limited to our personal lives. Organizations spend billions of dollars every year on assessments, training, coaching, off-site retreats, and various educational programs to help employees improve and be more effective. Given the substantial investment, it's important to understand the factors that either facilitate or inhibit change and improvement. What can the individual and the organization do to increase the odds of success?

In this chapter, we will review the theoretical foundations of how individual contributors, managers, and executives can and do improve. We also will explore common barriers to improvement within the workplace. We will conclude by suggesting science-based approaches to overcome those barriers.

Theoretical foundations for improvement

Individual differences

When considering the best ways to improve, it can be helpful to consider the nature of individual differences. That is, in what ways do people differ and how do those differences impact an individual's ability to change or grow? Several theories bring to light many of the underpinnings and causes of human behavior. Whereas, some of these theories are well established and very large in scope (e.g., Social Learning Theory), others are much more on the cutting-edge (e.g., the neuroscience of leadership—an extension of Trait Theory).

These theories form the basis of a full spectrum of methodologies for individual improvement, ranging from cognitive therapy to the search for deep motives and unmet needs in psychoanalytic theory. Although the personal and somewhat invasive nature of some assessment methods based on these theories are clinically focused and therefore untenable for modern talent management practices, they do remind practitioners of the complex and, at times, inexplicable barriers that can hinder employee performance. Further, they provide a clear picture of why modifying human behavior can be so difficult. (See Table 1.)

Table 1. Summary of common theoretical models of individual differences

THEORY & AUTHOR(S)	INDIVIDUAL BEHAVIOR DEPENDS UPON	METHOD FOR CHANGING OR IMPROVING BEHAVIOR	LIMITATIONS OF THE THEORY
Social Learning Theory *Bandura;* *Pavlov;* *Thorndike*	History of rewards and punishments.	Practice and reward or punish behaviors.	• Ignores underlying motivation and meaning of behavior. • Assumes that all behavior can be shaped via rewards.
Trait Theory *Allport;* *Cattell*	Underlying neurological, genetic, or biochemical structures.	Assess and understand trait profiles and align with job and context.	• Focuses on which traits vary but not why. • Difficult to change crystallized traits. • In early stages of scientific exploration.
Psycho-Analytical Theory *Freud*	Repressed and unconscious feelings and responses.	Various assessment techniques and therapy.	• Difficult to assess. • Oversimplifies motivations for behavior. • Focuses on maladaptive responses.
Interpersonal Theory *Adler;* *Horney*	Responses to feelings of insecurities that arise from social interactions.	Identify and modify methods used to compensate for inadequacies.	• Ignores underlying traits. • Focuses on maladaptive responses.
Humanistic Theory *Jung;* *Maslow*	Level of self-actualization and blocks in environment.	Establish stage of self-actualization and eliminate blocks.	• Success benchmark is self-determined. • Nature of the process is self-centered and contrary to society and organizations.

Table 1. Continued

THEORY & AUTHOR(S)	INDIVIDUAL BEHAVIOR DEPENDS UPON	METHOD FOR CHANGING OR IMPROVING BEHAVIOR	LIMITATIONS OF THE THEORY
Personal Construct Theory *Kelly*	Development and interpretation of cognitive theories.	Make personal theories explicit; shape theories.	• Theories are idiosyncratic and hard to assess and compare.
Socio-Analytical Theory *Hogan*	Need for social interactions; early experiences in groups; personal theories.	External observation and feedback of behaviors used within social system.	• Focuses on external observations, ignoring internal affective states which may be important for motivation and engagement.

Other research has investigated individual qualities that influence a person's desire and ability to change. For example, if a person is achievement oriented or highly motivated, they will likely have a strong desire to improve and change. Other qualities involve the ability or capacity to change. For example, learning agility (the ability to learn from new experiences) enables an individual to let go of old patterns of behavior and adapt and learn from new experiences (Eichinger, Lombardo, & Capretta, 2010; De Meuse, Dai, & Hallenbeck, 2010). The desire (motivation) to change and the ability (capacity) to change are interdependent. Willingness to change does not automatically bring about improvement—a person must be able to change. Likewise, ability to change does not guarantee improvement—a person must also be willing and motivated to change. (See Table 2.)

|

Table 2. Research-based individual qualities impacting improvement

	INDIVIDUAL QUALITY	DEFINITION	IMPACT ON IMPROVEMENT
DESIRE FOR CHANGE	Need for achievement	Need to excel according to set standards.	Higher need for achievement relates with desire to improve process or outcomes.
	Motivation	Intensity, direction, and persistence to attain a goal.	Fundamental to any improvement effort.
	Engagement	Mindset of taking responsibility for organizational success.	Exerts discretionary effort to help organizational goals.
	Conscientiousness	Responsibility, dependability, persistence, organized.	Concern for details, impact on others, and feedback.
	Openness to experience	Curiosity, imagination, sensitivity.	High openness means more willing to try new strategies and novel experiences. Low openness means a desire to stay within comfort zone.
	Goal orientation	Personal theory on goal setting and attainment.	Learning goal orientation will be more willing to test strengths and face novel situations. Performance orientation uses proven strengths and avoids mistakes.
	Locus of control	Belief that one is either impacted predominantly by internal or external factors.	Internal locus will lead to openness to feedback and efforts to improve. External locus will lead to defensiveness and desire to maintain status quo.
	Belief in change	Belief in one's capacity and resources to change and that change is worthwhile.	Positive beliefs will help one see beyond comfort and unknowns. Negative beliefs will focus on maintaining current state.
	Feedback orientation	Openness to information on behavior or performance.	Positive orientation seeks and acts on feedback. Negative orientation avoids situations in which failure is visible.

Table 2. Continued

	INDIVIDUAL QUALITY	DEFINITION	IMPACT ON IMPROVEMENT
CAPACITY TO CHANGE	Learning agility	Ability to learn from experiences and apply learning to novel situations.	Those high in learning agility are more likely to seek feedback and improve. Those low in learning agility may require more coaching, feedback, and more planful, structured learning opportunities.
	Emotional intelligence (EQ)	Ability to detect and manage emotional cues and information.	High EQ increases perception of impact of faults on others. Low EQ may be more defensive and less able to determine need for change.
	Self-efficacy	Belief that one is capable; self-confidence.	High self-efficacy leads to willingness to take on more challenges and ambiguity. Low self-efficacious individuals shy away from unknowns and untested skill areas.
	Cognitive load capacity	Capacity for amount of information that can be processed.	Greater capacity means more able to process emotional and cognitive stimuli, and reflect and learn. Lower capacity means more likely to be overwhelmed and avoid improvement.

Situational variables

In addition to individual differences and qualities, there are situational or environmental variables that impact improvement efforts. Research has investigated factors that highlight the individual's need to change as well as factors that create a work environment that encourages and supports individual improvement. For example, when an individual is held to clear performance targets or sees the prospect of career advancement, these factors can prompt an individual to change and improve. When the need to change is coupled with a positive manager relationship, organizational support, and challenging work, the possibility that change and improvement will occur increases dramatically. (See Table 3.)

Table 3. Research-based situational variables impacting improvement

	SITUATIONAL VARIABLE	DEFINITION	IMPACT ON IMPROVEMENT
NEED FOR CHANGE	Performance targets	Personal, team, and organizational goals.	Can foster the adoption of an improvement plan in order to increase contribution and exceed goals.
	Career stage and ambition	Motivation and desire to move up the corporate ladder.	High ambition leads to making things happen by developing and marketing oneself.
	Promotion	Moving up levels changes which skills are important.	Challenges current state and skill level to prevent derailment.
	Failure	Threats of demotion or termination.	Pending or past failures provide great impetus to change, moving individuals beyond inertia into action.
WORK ENVIRONMENT	Manager relationship	Immediate supervisor.	One of strongest factors impacting success of improvement, as the manager is the primary source of feedback, opportunities, and rewards.
	Environmental change	Agile or constantly changing organization.	Forces individuals to face novel situations and ambiguity.
	Organizational support	Level of support or resources available to the individual.	Perception of support fosters increased willingness to take risks.
	Organizational culture	Values, norms, and attitudes within the organization.	Culture of learning, accountability, and transparency create an atmosphere of trust, safety, and sincerity in goal setting.
	Nature of the work	Characteristics of job tasks, requirements, and working conditions.	Directs the feasibility and potential success of certain improvement plans.
	Size and structure of organization	Number of divisions, global reach, number of levels.	Drives the number and types of resources and developmental opportunities available.

Barriers to improving individual performance

Naturally, some attempts at individual improvement do work. However, given the complexities of people and the intricacies of organizations, not all improvement plans work across all individuals and within all companies (Dragoni, Tesluk, & Russell, 2009; Lord & Hall, 2005). There are many individual and organizational factors that can block or enhance personal development. What do we know about the causes of these failures? What are the barriers to improvement? In this section, we describe three types of barriers: (1) individual barriers, (2) organizational barriers, and (3) barriers related to the improvement process itself.

Individual barriers to improvement

Every individual possesses a unique array of characteristics and behavioral tendencies that can chill the improvement process. Some of these barriers can stifle an individual's willingness to make changes. Others are related to personality, which are less malleable. Some barriers related to the individual include the following:

Individuals tend to avoid painful realities. People do not like bad personal news. Whether the "pain" may be due to a sense of rejection or wounds to one's ego, negative feedback can be followed by little change in performance or the abandonment of work-related goals, especially when individuals reject the feedback (Atwater & Brett, 2005). On the other hand, evidence suggests that individuals facing clear, concrete, and undeniable negative consequences are likely to put substantial effort into responding to feedback (Lawler, 2003).

Individuals tend to be addicts of their own personalities. People tend to do activities in the manner they always have performed them. Individuals often are on autopilot. Individuals frequently try to deny the gap between present and required skills, failing to take the necessary action to reduce that gap (DeRue & Wellman, 2009). It is sometimes only when faced with the most challenging (beyond their current level of skills) work tasks or assignments that individuals will think more positively about moving outside of their comfort zone and the status quo (Bardwick, 1995).

The "knowing-doing gap." It is not enough to know that change must take place; individuals must be motivated to take action and then act. There can be several reasons why individuals do not take the necessary steps (Pfeffer & Sutton, 2000). They could be relying on their existing (outmoded) practices, accepting faulty underlying assumptions, or may be distrusting the organization's motives for suggesting change (Wanous, Reichers, & Austin, 2000). Even if all the supportive organizational resources are in place and there exists a motivation to change, individuals still may decide not to change. In cases where the change is not rewarded, they might conclude that improving the behavior or performance is not worth their effort, time, and energy.

|

Organizational barriers to individual improvement

The success of an individual's improvement plan also is affected by various factors within the organization. Some barriers can be changed or eliminated. Others force modifications to the improvement process itself. We highlight a few key barriers below.

Failed manager-subordinate or coaching relationships. Good managers and effective coaches spend less time examining the past and more time focusing on the future. Naturally, it is important to review why performance was unacceptable or what caused poor behavior to occur. However, dwelling too much on the past can create a sense of distrust between the manager and the employee. The past is history; it is over. The employee cannot change the past. The primary reason for discussing past failure is to learn from it. When a manager or coach focuses too much attention on past failures, it can impede improvement by lowering employee motivation and engagement (Kaiser & Kaplan, 2006).

Lack of regular feedback or data. Employees depend on reinforcement when they have performed correctly and expect a constructive critique of their work to help them be more effective (Lawler, 2003). Lack of feedback perpetuates performance ignorance, siloed processes, and flawed decision making. It also inhibits learning (DeRue & Wellman, 2009). Best-in-class organizations utilize frequent employee feedback in the form of annual performance reviews, 360° feedback programs, mentorship activities, coaching, and ongoing dialogue with the immediate manager ("Best practices," 2006). This information increases self-awareness and can help individuals reconcile contradictory perspectives of their performance.

Wrong types of goals. Research shows that setting the proper mix of goals can directly impact the success of the improvement process. "Learning goals" should focus on developing the right thinking processes to acquire knowledge and strategies for impacting individual, team, and organizational outcomes. In contrast, "outcome goals" are more prescriptive, guiding individuals to learn new procedures and tasks. Individuals also can set "performance goals" related to job attainment objectives. It is important to understand that not all goals are directly associated with performance improvement (Dragoni, Tesluk, & Russell, 2009; Seijts & Latham, 2006).

Limited accountability. Research demonstrates that having a system of accountability can greatly enhance the effectiveness of improvement plans. Individuals who have less ongoing support for the change process tend to make significantly fewer strides in improvement (Smither, London, & Reilly, 2005). Organizations that achieve best-in-class profiles emphasize making performance improvement a significant part of the organizational culture via visibility, communication, and accountability (Saba & Bourke, 2010).

Barriers related to the improvement process itself

Individuals work in demanding and evolving organizational systems. Consequently, the improvement process must be fluid and flexible to match the adaptive nature of the organization's environment and the readiness and motivation of individuals. Several barriers related to the selection and implementation of improvement plans also need to be considered.

Trying to improve too much at once. Individuals have limits to the amount of change they can handle at one time. Change brings with it stress. Research reveals that an individual's degree of arousal in brain activity increases when facing unfamiliar or intense stimuli (DeRue & Wellman, 2009). Hence, individuals are forced to turn their attention onto dealing with emotional responses to tasks. In essence, there may be a law of diminishing returns once an experience achieves a certain heightened level of intensity or risk, as in a challenging work assignment. As a result, trying to change too much or too quickly may be counterproductive.

Attempting to focus on the most difficult area to change first. Not all skills or competencies are created equal when it comes to improvement. For example, interpersonal skills generally represent one of the most fundamentally difficult skill sets to change (Hogan & Warrenfeltz, 2003). Lombardo and Eichinger (2001) have rigorously and methodically calibrated the developmental difficulty of the 67 competencies in the Leadership Architect® Library. While individuals consistently improve more on easier-to-develop competencies, it can be encouraging to note that even small improvements on difficult skills needed for job performance can have a huge impact (Dai, De Meuse, & Peterson, 2010). However, improper alignment of the developmental difficulty level and an individual's capacity for change can result in the employee abandoning the change effort altogether or diminishing an employee's willingness to improve that weakness at a later time (Moen & Allgood, 2009).

Focusing on strengths alone. Popular in some circles, the strengths-based development movement suggests that the most effective way to develop managers is to identify and develop strengths (Buckingham & Clifton, 2001). However, relying too heavily on one's strengths is a key cause of executive derailment (Eichinger, Dai, & Tang, 2009). Too much focus on strengths also may inhibit growth by reducing exposure to challenging, novel experiences.

In response to all the possible barriers to improvement, many companies provide limited solutions, such as suggesting a sole type of developmental plan or focusing only on strengths. In reality, there are many ways to improve— this book reviews 14 paths to improvement.

Effective approaches to improving individual performance

When we consider the approaches which are most effective in helping individuals improve, three areas of research are most salient to examine. Initially, we will briefly review the effect of 360° feedback programs. Subsequently, we will investigate the impact of executive coaching. Finally, we will explore a model of individual development and improvement.

360° Feedback

Close to 90% of the Fortune 1000 companies use 360° or multi-rater feedback (Brutus et al., 2006). There is evidence that 360° feedback heightens self-awareness and has a positive impact on performance (e.g., Church & Waclawski, 1999). Further, combining these 360° assessments with development plans has been found to improve performance by a number of researchers (Green, 2002; Thach, 2002; Smither, London, Flautt, Vargas, & Kucine, 2003). However, some studies have found minimal or less direct benefits (Bailey & Austin, 2006; Seifert, Yukl, & McDonald, 2003). Other studies have found that *lower* performers tend to show more improvement after multi-rater assessments than *higher* performers (Reilly, Smither, & Vasilopoulos, 1996). Many of the studies finding limited or lack of support of the effectiveness of these assessments note a number of methodological problems, including the difficulty of rating the multi-dimensional nature of performance, not accounting for the various levels of leadership competency difficulty, and using only a composite measure of performance improvement rather than assessing improvement on selected competencies for development.

A study attempted to address some of these problems. Dai, De Meuse, and Peterson (2010) investigated specific changes in skill ratings on 67 competencies at four times over 12 years and accounted for competency developmental difficulty. During this period, each manager selected several competencies bottom-ranked on skill but top-ranked on importance. For these competencies, managers engaged in developmental activities identified on an individual development plan (IDP) devised with assistance from an internal coach. Progress on the IDP activities was scored and linked with recognition and rewards. As predicted, the results indicated that managers significantly improved more on the competencies selected for development than on competencies not selected. It also was found that improvement continued over time but eventually leveled off. Finally, Dai and his colleagues observed that improvement was negatively correlated with developmental difficulty, suggesting that managers made less improvement on the harder-to-develop competencies than on the easier ones. Overall, the findings demonstrated that multi-source feedback in conjunction with enacted individual development plans had a positive and sustained impact on performance improvement.

Coaching

Another line of research has focused on the effectiveness of coaching. Similar to the use of 360° feedback, coaching has become very prominent within leadership development practices around the world (Corporate Leadership Council, 2003). Across multiple studies, coaching has been demonstrated to moderate the relationship between assessment and performance improvement (Green, 2002; Thach, 2002). In addition, Luthans and Peterson (2003) reported that work attitudes improved following feedback-coaching interventions. In a meta-analysis of empirical studies examining coaching effectiveness, De Meuse, Dai, and Lee (2009) found that executive coaching had a positive effect on both skill and performance ratings. Additionally, within the same study, the authors revealed that coaching was *perceived* to have a significant impact on business results and provide a positive return on investment (ROI), but no scientific evidence was found to support it.

Overall, the empirical literature strongly suggests that 360° feedback as well as coaching can significantly enhance performance improvement for individuals. The extent of improvement likely is affected by many factors. Both individual and organizational variables can come into play.

The $A^3B^2C^1$ Growth and coaching model

In addition to receiving multi-rater feedback and coaching, it can be helpful for individuals and coaches to have a model that leads them through the improvement process. One of the most relevant models of individual development and improvement is the $A^3B^2C^1$ Growth and coaching model (Lombardo & Eichinger, 2004). This model posits that development is not an event but a process—a process of six specific steps. Whether the goal is self-improvement or coaching someone else, the six-step process is a how-to guide for individual improvement.

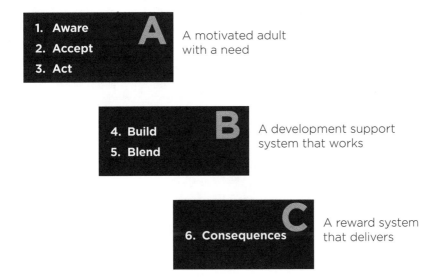

1. **Aware**
2. **Accept**
3. **Act**

A — A motivated adult with a need

4. **Build**
5. **Blend**

B — A development support system that works

6. **Consequences**

C — A reward system that delivers

| 81

A – Awareness, Acceptance, Action

The *A* stage of the model is *Awareness, Acceptance,* and *Action*. Individuals aren't likely to improve in an area of need if they have no idea that it is something they should be working on. The majority of people have at least one blind spot—an area where they believe they are doing OK but others see a lot of room for improvement. Gaining *awareness* that a need to improve exists is the first step. Next, an individual must *accept* and take personal responsibility for the need. The core issue of this step is to work through defensiveness. The source of defensiveness may need to be addressed more than once in order to move on to the next stage. In order to *act,* the learner needs to be motivated to do something about the need (Lombardo & Eichinger, 2004). As a coach, your role is critical for this to occur. There are several approaches to working through obstacles to building motivation and taking action, including rewards and consequences. Whatever technique one uses, the goal is to give the individual a compelling reason to change.

B – Build and Blend

The *B* stage of the model addresses the *Build* and *Blend* steps. A motivated learner with a need is ready to *build* a plan that works. There are some important factors to consider. How much time can be allocated to address the need? How long will it take for real signs of improvement to begin? What aspects in the work environment might distract from implementing new approaches or reinforce current practices? Another issue to consider in this step is that development is not always about taking a straight line to "get better" at something. Often, more indirect and creative approaches can be used. We may have engendered the motivation and the plan, but we also need to execute. Now, we have arrived at the *blend* step. Important elements here are encouragement, feedback, a willingness to tolerate mistakes, and being open to experimentation. The plan for development, no matter how well crafted, does not always meet our expectations. Problems need to be identified and diagnosed early, alternatives explored, and new approaches monitored for effectiveness. Leveraging others for feedback, advice, and support is particularly helpful.

C – Consequences

After the first five steps have been implemented successfully, the final step to manage—the *C*—is *Consequences*. When a developmental goal has been accomplished, make sure the desired rewards are delivered and celebrate the achievement. If efforts have fallen short, take a hard look at what did not go right and consider other *consequences*. Either way, an accounting of the process needs to take place and the appropriate outcomes delivered. This provides closure and sets the stage for subsequent developmental efforts.

There is much theoretical support for the $A^3B^2C^1$ Growth and coaching model (e.g., reinforcement theory, social learning theory). A key facet of this model is awareness—whether it is achieved via feedback from a boss, a 360° survey, or a coach. For improvement to occur, individuals must be cognizant that change (improvement) is needed. Although this point might seem obvious, research indicates the majority of individual contributors, managers, and executives have at least one blind spot (Orr, Swisher, Tang, & De Meuse, 2010). Ultimately, the combination of the three approaches discussed in this section—360° feedback, coaching, and a model for improvement—can greatly increase the probability of success when it comes to individual improvement efforts.

Concluding remarks

While it is not easy to change and improve, it is possible. Research and the experiences of personal trainers and executive coaches bear witness to the complex realities embedded in trying to change human behavior. The theoretical foundations of individual differences depict many underlying mechanisms, motives, and processes that drive behavior. Likewise, many barriers within an individual and organization can impede improvement.

Yet, it remains critical for individuals to improve and for organizations to assist them in these efforts. Fortunately, research suggests there are many things that can facilitate individual development. The use of 360° feedback can enhance self-awareness. Coaches and mentors can be of great assistance in helping individuals grow and evolve. Individuals are not left to gamble on fads or self-help books. People can and do change, and there are science-based plans to assist them in navigating through the intricate mazes of improvement.

How to select plans

How to select the best plan involves the individual's awareness, acceptance, willingness to take action, and whether it makes sense to build skill directly. The following decision tree takes you through a series of questions to help determine which plan will be most helpful and effective for the individual you are coaching.

Figure 1. How to select the best plan

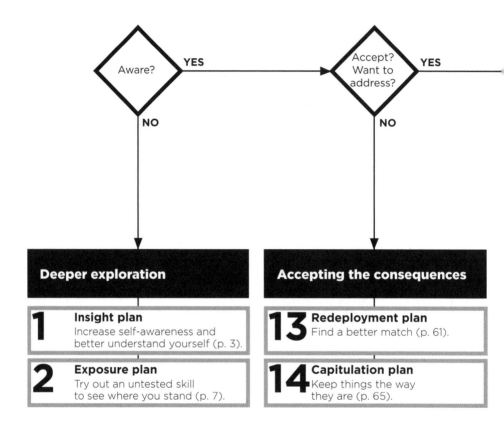

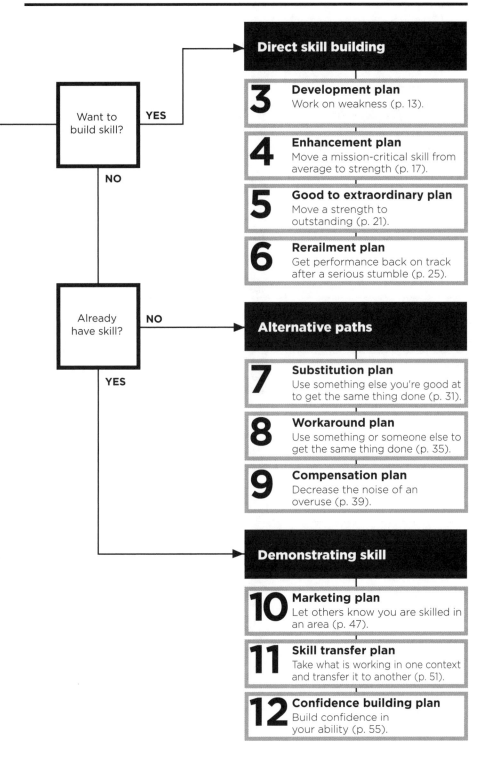

Direct skill building

3 **Development plan**
Work on weakness (p. 13).

4 **Enhancement plan**
Move a mission-critical skill from average to strength (p. 17).

5 **Good to extraordinary plan**
Move a strength to outstanding (p. 21).

6 **Rerailment plan**
Get performance back on track after a serious stumble (p. 25).

Want to build skill? — **YES**

NO

Already have skill? — **NO**

YES

Alternative paths

7 **Substitution plan**
Use something else you're good at to get the same thing done (p. 31).

8 **Workaround plan**
Use something or someone else to get the same thing done (p. 35).

9 **Compensation plan**
Decrease the noise of an overuse (p. 39).

Demonstrating skill

10 **Marketing plan**
Let others know you are skilled in an area (p. 47).

11 **Skill transfer plan**
Take what is working in one context and transfer it to another (p. 51).

12 **Confidence building plan**
Build confidence in your ability (p. 55).

In Table 4, we provide some additional information on the features of each of the 14 paths to improvement, including the time frame, the degree of coaching support needed, and the likelihood that you will see improvement.

Table 4. Paths to improvement features

Paths to improvement	Time frame	Degree of coaching support	Likelihood you'll see improvement
Deeper exploration			
1. Insight plan	◔	Moderate	Low
2. Exposure plan	◔	Moderate	Moderate
Direct skill building			
3. Development plan	◕	Moderate	Low
4. Enhancement plan	◑	High	High
5. Good to extraordinary plan	◑	High	Moderate
6. Rerailment plan	●	High	Low
Alternative paths			
7. Substitution plan	◔	Moderate	Moderate
8. Workaround plan	◔	Low	High
9. Compensation plan	◔	Moderate	Moderate
Demonstrating skill			
10. Marketing plan	◑	Low	High
11. Skill transfer plan	◑	Low	High
12. Confidence building plan	◕	Low	Moderate
Accepting the consequences			
13. Redeployment plan	◑	Low	Moderate
14. Capitulation plan	◔	Low	Low

◔ = Shorter time frame   ● = Longer time frame

Coaching notes

When you sit down for a coaching conversation, you will be able to tell very quickly whether you are working with a curious, willing participant in the coaching process or whether you are up against a defensive, stubborn opponent. The former takes immediate responsibility and ownership; the latter won't accept reality regardless of the amount of evidence. Most individuals fall somewhere in between.

When you fail to see any progress in a reasonable amount of time, or if the individual responds in unexpected ways, recognize that there may be deeper issues at play. Few bosses or even coaches are trained to handle and fix deeper problems. Refer the person to more skilled resources who can provide the appropriate professional help.

Deeper exploration

1 Insight plan

Increase self-awareness and better understand yourself (p. 3).

In order to improve effectiveness, raise performance, or enhance career options, an individual needs to be ready for honest self-examination. Before an individual can take action and improve in an area of need, they must be aware of the need. Becoming self-aware may not be comfortable, but it's the first step toward improvement. Awareness can come from the outside in (feedback) or the inside out (personal reflection). The next critical step is acceptance—the individual needs to be receptive to the feedback and acknowledge that it has merit. Awareness and acceptance of a need paves the way for an individual to change and improve.

Be prepared for coaching and feedback conversations filled with skepticism, guardedness, and possibly defensiveness, resistance, and conflict. You are providing a wake-up call about the gaps in perception, revealing blind spots or potential derailers. It is very important to find out "the why" behind the differences in perception. Many times it's "the why" that points to "the what" to do. Your job is to build awareness, help the person gain additional insight, and possibly have a breakthrough.

2 Exposure plan

Try out an untested skill to see where you stand (p. 7).

It's important to involve the boss, as this person is often a gatekeeper for exposure opportunities. When thinking about an Exposure plan, it's wise to start small. Keep the plan low risk. Get an initial estimate of how skilled learners are by starting small and working up to more significant challenges. You don't want someone to go into a high-risk situation in order to test a skill—where there's a good chance they don't really have it—if there's a lot riding on having a strength in that area. Or if the risk is high and the person still wants to forge ahead to prove something, you can help by thinking through a contingency plan. Thinking through the various scenarios and potential outcomes can help you establish a safety net.

Direct skill building

3 Development plan

Work on a weakness (p. 13).

Development is one of the hardest areas to address in a feedback session because it's the one most likely to trigger defense scripts. People naturally don't want to hear that others think they're bad at things, particularly those things that are important. And, of course, until someone is ready to plan for change—which is often two whole steps away from simply getting information—development planning is futile. When you encounter this, consider starting the individual off with an Insight plan. On the other hand, if the individual is aware and accepts their weakness in the mission-critical area and motivated to take action, then the Development plan is more likely to be beneficial.

Consider how difficult it is to develop the skill in question. If it is a skill that is easier to develop (like Planning or Informing), the Development plan can be completed in a shorter time frame. If the skill is more difficult to develop (like Innovation management or Conflict management), then it will be important to take a longer-range view. If possible, look ahead to the skills that are hard to develop and will be important in the future—encourage the individual to begin developing these skills early.

Keep in mind the 70:20:10 guidelines for skill development (McCall, Lombardo, & Morrison, 1988). Over the course of a person's career, typically 70% of significant learning experiences happen on the job; 20% of significant lessons are learned from observing and listening to others; and 10% of significant learning comes from coursework. This ratio does not discount the importance of formal education, training courses, or leadership development courses— these provide a crucial foundation upon which to build. However, the learning that happens as a result of real, on-the-job experiences is unrivaled.

When identifying full-time or part-time on-the-job development experiences, there are four factors that are important to consider: variety, intensity, diversity, and adversity. Over the course of a person's career, the more varied, risky, different, and difficult jobs and responsibilities they can experience, the more opportunity there will be for deep development.

Your job as coach may include encouraging an individual to take an assignment that does not seem appealing but is one that ultimately will be a very developmental assignment. Going against the grain—or GAG assignments—include assignments that an individual would not seek out or self-select into. Highlight the features of the assignment that are most developmental and point out the potential developmental payoffs.

4 Enhancement plan
Move a mission-critical skill from average to a strength (p. 17).

The typical feedback system has traditionally focused mostly on fixing weaknesses. But people are more resistant to improving weaknesses. You're less likely to encounter resistance from an individual when you start out addressing those areas in which performance is already at least average because there is less threat for either of you to confront.

When you help the individual build an Enhancement plan, there are two potential benefits: (1) When you're successful in training average performers in the real behaviors of superior performers in specific jobs, they often increase skill fairly quickly, and the increase can be measured in real profit and sales increases. (2) Once the planning session is moving in a positive direction and the individual is optimistically thinking about improvement, it will be easier to focus on "the bad news" and begin to mitigate weaknesses.

5 Good to extraordinary plan
Move a strength to outstanding (p. 21).

You might be familiar with the concepts and findings in Jim Collins' book *Good to Great*. One of the key findings—and it comes as no surprise—is that companies that made the transition from good to great performers had the most effective leaders as well as strong succession processes.

We also know from research that there are significant organizational performance gains to be realized when HR practices are integrated around a competency model aligned to the strategic plan of the business (Becker, Huselid, & Beatty, 2009). With such an aligned competency model, you know what the mission-critical areas of focus are for the leaders you are coaching. And with the information from feedback, it's easy to tell where further opportunities for improvement lie.

Remember, with a Good to extraordinary plan, you're dealing with someone who is, by all accounts, a high performer and in the high potential pool. The intent in this case will be to use feedback as a springboard to turbocharge this person's overall performance by focusing on moving strengths to towering strengths.

It might be tough to convince someone who is already talented that they should continue to develop. You can easily cite any number of star athletes who continue to take lessons and get coaching. High performers who don't stop learning have the potential to break their own records.

It is important to watch out for overused strengths. There are two common situations where you will see this occur: (1) when an individual is not able to discern changing direction, strategies, or responsibilities that require a different approach and a different set of skills, and (2) when things are not going as planned or when the individual is stretched and their approach is to turn up the volume on strengths that have helped deliver results in the past. It is possible to have too much of a good thing. If you see signs of overuse, turn to the Compensation plan on page 39.

6 **Rerailment plan**
Get performance back on track after a serious stumble (p. 25).

There are a few challenges that you as a coach are likely to encounter when working with someone who is derailing. Primary among these is defensiveness (and you should be aware of the multiple defense scripts that people engage to shield themselves from the pain of truth). Depending on the nature and degree of the problem, you may find more or less resistance. One common defense script is to minimize the harmfulness of the problem. Consider, for instance, how arrogance might be tolerated in certain situations or organizations but not in others. It also gets called "high standards" or "intelligence" or "deeply skilled behaviors."

Consider whether there are logical connections you can make between overuse of strengths and strong stallers and stoppers. Sometimes they are simply flip sides of the same coin. What is the relationship, for instance, between overusing strengths such as Priority setting, Directing others, or Planning and the staller we call Overmanaging? Is it only in its impact on others? Or on one's own career?

Keep in mind that the organization stands to benefit if you are able to assist the derailing individual in making a turnaround. Remember, these are not people who are considered dispensable; they are usually high achievers with a track record of success, and getting them back on track is not only cheaper than replacing them, but you're also going to find that those who have been saved from derailing become strong advocates for the development process that saved them.

Depending on the situation, consider suggesting the following approaches to the derailing individual:

- Get a more accurate self-assessment to increase self-awareness (this can take time to develop).
- Gain a better understanding of the derailment process.
- Get outside help.
- Consider redeployment (perhaps temporary).

To successfully employ a Rerailment plan requires deep coaching expertise and experience. Don't hesitate to seek coaching yourself in order to increase the odds of helping an individual alter their behavior and thereby avoid being fired, demoted, or stalled.

Alternative paths

7 Substitution plan
Use something else you're good at to get the same thing done (p. 31).

When helping someone create a Substitution plan, much as you would when looking at a workaround strategy, be sure to take both a near-term and long-term view (a job view and a career view). When someone is looking at substitutions for a weakness, they should also be thinking about how to develop that need over the longer term. Identifying what skills to become better at to achieve their career goals will help guide decisions about where to invest in development versus where to focus on finding a substitute.

A Substitution plan is smart and efficient. Not everyone needs to be good at everything. A Substitution plan is not a cop-out if the person has other strengths on the mission-critical list, is comfortable being weak in a key area, and through the Substitution plan gets things done as well as, or better than, before. That is, the Substitution plan worked. Understanding how to do a Substitution plan can actually be thought of as a skill. There is probably a limit to how many weaknesses the person can and should cover with Substitution plans, but as long as they get things done and there are other resources available to do that, it's smart.

8 Workaround plan
Use someone or something else to get the same thing done (p. 35).

A note of caution: It is critical that the individual knows what their weaknesses are. It's one thing to work around them, and another to simply ignore them or underestimate their impact. As a coach, you can help the individual assess how important the skill is to success in the job. Also, assess the degree to which the weakness is creating problems. Make sure that it hasn't crossed over into negative behavior that could impede job performance and career progress. If you would flag it as a potential career staller, consider applying the Rerailment plan (see page 25).

Some managers or organizations will not like the idea of working around a weakness. In a culture that has embraced individual development plans, the Workaround plan may seem like an avoidance tactic. Be sensitive to this perspective and make sure that the individual is in fact focused on developing skills in other areas.

A Workaround plan is smart and efficient. Not everyone needs to be good at everything. A Workaround plan is not a cop-out if the person has other strengths on the mission-critical list, is comfortable being weak in a key area, and through the Workaround plan gets things done as well as, or better than, before. That is, the Workaround plan worked. Understanding how to do a Workaround plan can actually be thought of as a skill. There is probably a limit to how many weaknesses the person can and should cover with Workaround plans, but as long as they get things done and there are other resources available to do that, it's smart.

9 Compensation plan
Decrease the noise of an overuse (p. 39).

The solution seems obvious and straightforward: ease off the throttle. But there are times when it's fruitless to argue with success or to try to refute logic. Remember, the person you're coaching may have gotten where they are in the organization based on those strengths.

When you're dealing with overused strengths, be prepared to confront some aggressive defensiveness. If you haven't already done so, it will be helpful to gather some feedback. You might consider using a 360° feedback survey that allows raters to indicate potential overuse when they are rating the competencies.

Work with those you coach to help them discover what has caused a given strength to kick into overdrive. Help them develop the insight to know when to step up their use of other skills. *FYI® For Your Improvement* 5th Edition will be a helpful reference tool for what overuse looks like, what some root causes might be, and for a list of compensators that can mitigate overuse in any of the 67 leadership skills. Having the behavioral indicators, possible causes, and ready-to-implement solutions can help the individual acknowledge and accept feedback related to an overused strength.

Demonstrating skill

10 Marketing plan
Let others know you are skilled in an area (p. 47).

The Marketing plan is one of the easiest plans to execute, and there is usually a very high return on effort. The challenge for you is to determine whether the individual you are coaching truly is as skilled as they claim.

If you have the benefit of a 360° feedback report, you will notice a look of surprise when someone gets rated lower than they were expecting on a skill. It is your job to assess whether this is a blind spot (the individual lacks awareness of a weakness) or if this is a case where the individual is not getting credit for their ability.

To determine this, you will need some proof that the individual possesses the skill. You can approach the conversation as you might approach a behavioral interview. Ask for examples to illustrate when and how they demonstrated the skill. Develop an understanding of the situation described, the actions taken, the thinking behind it, the outcomes, and the degree to which learning has been applied to current situations. Listen for positive or negative themes that help indicate the individual's skill level.

If you become convinced that the individual is skilled and that the difference of opinion is simply a gap in perception, then the Marketing plan is an appropriate path.

11 Skill transfer plan
Take what is working in one context and transfer it to another (p. 51).

As a coach, when you discover a need or a weakness, before going down the development path, always ask, "Do you do this well or better anywhere else in your life or work?"

Many times people will tell you about doing it well in church, among friends, in social settings, in volunteer work, with customers, or even at home.

In the Skill transfer approach, you will want to help the person clearly see the skills they initiate in a non-work setting and how to apply those skills at work. It's as simple as taking out a legal pad, drawing a line down the center, and on one side describing (listing) what they do to successfully display a skill in one context, then listing what that would look like at work. In order to transfer those skills, help the person remove the attitudinal or other barriers to applying the skills in another context. The line you have drawn will disappear.

12 Confidence building plan
Build confidence in your ability (p. 55).

There is a burning need to build confidence in individuals whose performance is limited by a lack of self-confidence in one or more areas. Individuals with hidden strengths are less likely to fully utilize them. They may be reticent to seek out challenges because they lack confidence. These individuals are less likely to reach their full potential and contribute their utmost to the organization.

Getting at the root cause for their lack of confidence is the most valuable way you can help. It's important in this plan to know why they underestimate their skills because the reasons will generally lead to what to do about it.

Keep in mind areas where individuals frequently underestimate their ability. One study looked at the most common hidden strengths among leaders. The study found that managing up, understanding the business, making complex decisions, and being organizationally savvy were the most common areas where individuals rated themselves significantly lower in skill than others (Orr, Swisher, Tang, & De Meuse, 2010).

Accepting the consequences

13 Redeployment plan
Find a better match (p. 61).

Tread lightly in these conversations. People who are ready to admit defeat in a particular job or organization are most likely feeling vulnerable. Be ready to engage the individual in some soul-searching conversations—a change of this magnitude brings up a lot of questions that require deep reflection.

Help the individual determine what the interim plan will be. If the redeployment process takes a few months, they will need to maintain a baseline level of performance in the current role. When appropriate, refer the individual to a career center or outplacement service if the individual needs critical resources that will help them navigate the career planning/job search process.

Redeployment is a reasonable and effective approach to staffing—getting the right people with the right skills in the right job.

96 |

14 Capitulation plan
Keep things the way they are (p. 65).

You're more likely to encounter this type of response when the person you're coaching is closing in on the end of a career and is more or less biding time. You may also face it with someone who is truly burned out and has decided to give up. Or you may face it with someone who is a stellar performer but thinks their performance justifies bad behavior.

Take time to explore options with the individual—it may be possible to steer them toward a different plan—like a Redeployment plan or a Workaround plan. View capitulation as a last resort.

That said, be honest about likely consequences. Maybe nothing dramatic will change, maybe it will. Lay out the best-case and worst-case scenarios together so that the individual goes into it with their eyes open.

References

Atwater, L. E., & Brett, J. F. (2005). Antecedents and consequences of reactions to developmental 360 degree feedback. *Journal of Vocational Behavior, 66*(3), 532-548.

Bailey, C., & Austin, M. (2006). 360 Degree feedback and developmental outcomes: The role of feedback characteristics, self-efficacy and importance of feedback dimensions to focal managers' current role. *International Journal of Selection and Assessment, 14*(1), 51-66. doi:10.1111/j.1468-2389.2006.00333.x

Bardwick, J. M. (1995). *Danger in the comfort zone: From boardroom to mailroom—How to break the entitlement habit that's killing American business* (2nd ed.). New York, NY: AMACOM.

Becker, B. E., Huselid, M. A., & Beatty, R. W. (2009). *The differentiated workforce: Transforming talent into strategic impact.* Boston: Harvard Business School Press.

Best practices for performance management. (2006, October). [Executive Briefing]. *HR Magazine, 51*(10), p. 16.

Brutus, S., Derayeh, M., Fletcher, C., Bailey, C., Velazquez, P., Shi, K., Simon, C., & Labath, V. (2006). Internationalization of multi-source feedback systems: A six-country exploratory analysis of 360-degree feedback. *International Journal of Human Resource Management, 17,* 1888-1906.

Buckingham, M., & Clifton, D. O. (2001). *Now, discover your strengths.* New York, NY: Free Press.

Church, A. H., & Waclawski, J. (1999, Spring). Influence behaviors and managerial effectiveness in lateral relations. *Human Resource Development Quarterly, 10*(1), 3-34. doi:10.1002/hrdq.3920100103

Collins, J. C. (2001). *Good to great: Why some companies make the leap...and others don't.* New York, NY: HarperCollins.

Corporate Leadership Council. (2003). *Maximizing returns on professional executive coaching.* Washington, DC: Author.

Dai, G., De Meuse, K. P., & Peterson, C. (2010). Impact of multi-source feedback on leadership competency development: A longitudinal field study. *Journal of Managerial Issues, 22,* 197-219.

De Meuse, K. P., Dai, G., & Hallenbeck, G. S., Jr. (2010). Learning agility: A construct whose time has come. *Consulting Psychology Journal: Practice and Research, 62*(2), 119-130. doi:10.1037/a0019988

De Meuse, K. P., Dai, G., & Lee, R. J. (2009). Evaluating the effectiveness of executive coaching: Beyond ROI? *Coaching: An International Journal of Theory, Research and Practice, 2*(2), 117-134. doi:10.1080/17521880902882413

DeRue, D. S., & Wellman, N. (2009). Developing leaders via experience: The role of developmental challenge, learning orientation, and feedback availability. *Journal of Applied Psychology, 94*(4), 859-875. doi:10.1037/a0015317

Dragoni, L., Tesluk, P. E., Russell, J. A., & Oh, I. (2009). Understanding managerial development: Integrating developmental assignments, learning orientation, and access to developmental opportunities in predicting managerial competencies. *Academy of Management Journal, 52*(4), 731-743.

Dunnette, M. D. (1966). Fads, fashions, and folderol in psychology. *American Psychologist, 21*(4), 343-352. doi:10.1037/h0023535

Eichinger, R. W., Dai, G., & Tang, K. Y. (2009). It depends upon what you mean by a strength. In R. B. Kaiser (Ed.), *The perils of accentuating the positive* (pp. 13-26). Tulsa, OK: Hogan Press.

Eichinger, R. W., Lombardo, M. M., & Capretta, C. (2010). *FYI® for learning agility.* Minneapolis, MN: Lominger International: A Korn Ferry Company.

Finkelstein, S., Whitehead, J., & Campbell, A. (2008). *Think again: Why good leaders make bad decisions and how to keep it from happening to you.* Boston, MA: Harvard Business School Press.

Green, B. (2002). Listening to leaders: Feedback on 360-degree feedback one year later. *Organization Development Journal, 20*(1), 8-17.

Hogan, R., & Warrenfeltz, R. (2003). Educating the modern manager. *Academy of Management Learning and Education, 2*(1), 74-84.

Kaiser, R. B., & Kaplan, R. E. (2006). Outgrowing sensitivities: The deeper work of executive development. *Academy of Management Learning and Education, 5,* 463-483.

Lawler, E. E., III. (2003). Reward practices and performance management system effectiveness. *Organizational Dynamics, 32*(4), 396-404.

Lombardo, M. (2004). *The patterns of effective managers.* Presented at the Lominger Users Conference, Scottsdale, AZ and Chicago, IL.

Lombardo, M. M., & Eichinger, R. W. (2004). *The leadership machine: Architecture to develop leaders for any future* (3rd ed.). Minneapolis, MN: Lominger International: A Korn Ferry Company.

Lombardo, M. M., & Eichinger, R. W. (2009). *FYI® for your improvement* (5th ed.). Minneapolis, MN: Lominger International: A Korn Ferry Company.

Lord, R. G., & Hall, R. J. (2005). Identity, deep structure and the development of leadership skill. *Leadership Quarterly, 16*(4), 591-615. doi:10.1016/j.leaqua.2005.06.003

Luthans, F., & Peterson, S. J. (2003). 360-Degree feedback with systematic coaching: Empirical analysis suggests a winning combination. *Human Resource Management, 42*(3), 243-256. doi:10.1002/hrm.10083

McCall, M. W., Lombardo, M. M., & Morrison, A. M. (1988). *The lessons of experience.* Lexington, MA: Lexington Books.

McGovern, J., Lindemann, M., Vergara, M., Murphy, S., Barker, L., & Warrenfeltz, R. (2001). Maximizing the impact of executive coaching: Behavioral change, organizational outcomes, and return on investment. *Manchester Review, 6*(1), 1-9.

Mintzberg, H. (2004). *Managers not MBAs: A hard look at the soft practice of managing and management development.* San Francisco, CA: Berrett-Koehler Publishers.

Moen, F., & Allgood, E. (2009). Coaching and the effect on self-efficacy. *Organization Development Journal, 27*(4), 69-82.

Orr, J. E., Swisher, V. V., Tang, K. Y., & De Meuse, K. P. (2010). *Illuminating blind spots and hidden strengths* [White paper]. New York, NY: Korn Ferry Institute.

Parker-Wilkins, V. (2006). Business impact of executive coaching: Demonstrating monetary value. *Industrial and Commercial Training, 38*(3), 122-127. doi:10.1108/00197850610659373

Pfeffer, J., & Sutton, R. I. (2000). *The knowing-doing gap: How smart companies turn knowledge into action.* Boston, MA: Harvard Business School Press.

Reilly, R. R., Smither, J. W., & Vasilopoulos, N. L. (1996). A longitudinal study of upward feedback. *Personnel Psychology, 49*(3), 599-612. doi:10.1111/j.1744-6570.1996.tb01586.x

Ruyle, K. E., Hallenbeck, G. S., Jr., Orr, J. E., & Swisher, V. V. (2010). *FYI® for Insight: The 21 leadership characteristics for success and the 5 that get you fired.* Minneapolis, MN: Lominger International: A Korn Ferry Company.

Saba, J., & Bourke, J. (2010, May). *Employee performance management: The alpha and the omega of talent strategy and business execution.* Aberdeen Group. Retrieved from http://www.aberdeen.com/aberdeen-library/6361/RA-employee-performance-management.aspx.

Seifert, C. F., Yukl, G., & McDonald, R. A. (2003). Effects of multisource feedback and a feedback facilitator on the influence behavior of managers toward subordinates. *Journal of Applied Psychology, 88*(3), 561-569.

Seijts, G. H., & Latham, G. P. (2006, May/June). Learning goals or performance goals: Is it the journey or the destination? *Ivey Business Journal, 70,* 1-6.

Smither, J. W., London, M., Flautt, R., Vargas, Y., & Kucine, I. (2003). Can working with an executive coach improve multisource feedback ratings over time? A quasi-experimental field study. *Personnel Psychology, 56,* 23-44. doi:10.1111/j.1744-6570.2003.tb00142.x

Smither, J. W., London, M., & Reilly, R. R. (2005). Does performance improve following multisource feedback? A theoretical model, meta-analysis, and review of empirical findings. *Personnel Psychology, 58*(1), 33-66. doi:10.1111/j.1744-6570.2005.514_1.x

| 101

Thach, E. (2002). The impact of executive coaching and 360-degree feedback on leadership effectiveness. *Leadership and Organization Development Journal, 23*(4), 205-214. doi:10.1108/01437730210429070

Wanous, J. P., Reichers, A. E., & Austin, J. T. (2000). Cynicism about organizational change: Measurement, antecedents, and correlates. *Group & Organization Management, 25*(2), 132-153. doi:10.1177/1059601100252003

Zenger, J., & Folkman, J. (2002). *The extraordinary leader: Turning good managers into great leaders.* New York, NY: McGraw-Hill.